CUB SCOUTING

The First 75 Years of Doing Our Best

BOY SCOUTS OF AMERICA®

34473
ISBN 0-8395-4473-1

2005 Printing

Dedicated to

Tomorrow's boys of Cub Scout age

The families of those boys

The volunteer leaders in Cub Scouting

The professionals who work with Cub Scout leaders

—The National Cub Scout Committee

Contents

Foreword vi

Preface vii

Part A: The Story 1

Chapter 1—The Beginning: The BSA's Younger Boy Question 3

Chapter 2—The 1930s: Cub Scouting's Early Years 13

Chapter 3—The 1940s: Cub Scouting Comes of Age 25

Chapter 4—The 1950s: Taking Off 33

Chapter 5—The 1960s: Major Changes 41

Chapter 6—The 1970s: Broadening Cub Scouting's Reach 49

Chapter 7—1980: Cub Scouting's Golden Anniversary 59

Chapter 8—The 1980s: Program Expansion and the Introduction of Tiger Cubs 63

Chapter 9—The 1990s: A Decade Going Strong 75

Chapter 10—2000 and Beyond: Cub Scouting Moves Forward 85

Epilogue—The Challenge for the Future 95

Part B: The Appendix 99

Appendix 1—Major Events in Cub Scouting by Year 101

Appendix 2—Chief Scout Executives and Cub Scout Division Directors 111

Appendix 3—The Changing Role of Leaders 115

Index 119

Foreword

Every adventure has a beginning. For millions of young people across the nation and the world, the adventure of Scouting begins in Cub Scouting.

For 75 years, Cub Scouting has woven the lifetime values of good character, participating citizenship, and personal fitness into a fun and exciting program for youth. Former Cub Scouts of every generation carry with them fond memories of den meetings and outings filled with fun and friendship. What we don't realize until years later is that Cub Scouting laid the foundations of character and leadership that would shape the men we would become.

This very special book is a warm history of the program that played such an important role in our lives and the lives of our children. Just as importantly, it is an extraordinary tribute to those countless parents and volunteers who stepped forward to make a difference.

I hope you enjoy this book of Cub Scouting memories as much as I did.

Roy L. Williams
Chief Scout Executive

Preface

Since the beginning of the Cub Scout program in 1930, tens of millions of this country's youth and adult leaders have experienced the family adventure of Cub Scouting. No other educational youth movement can claim such achievements. These millions of volunteers and BSA professional staff leaders have contributed immeasurably to the program's success. Their spirit of dedication and voluntary commitment epitomizes Scouting's values and service to others.

As our history shows, Cub Scouting has built a solid foundation of service upon which future strengthening and improvement can and will create an even better program for youth. Our greatest objective is to meet the ever-changing needs of today's family to "Do Our Best" to "Be Prepared" for the family of tomorrow.

In 2005, Cub Scouting celebrates a major event: its Diamond Jubilee. Packs across the country and internationally will observe the program's 75th Anniversary with special activities.

Throughout the Diamond Jubilee celebration, from September 2004 through December 2005, we will learn much about Cub Scouting, locally and nationally. Special events will take place in every pack, district, and council. Cub Scouts will learn about citizenship, their communities, and the people who live there.

Shortly after the Golden Jubilee of Cub Scouting, celebrated during 1980, the *History of Cub Scouting* told the story of the first 50 years. This book draws upon those first five decades and continues the Cub Scouting story through the next 25 years. Many thanks to those who helped to create the first history book—Ann W. Nally and James D. Nally, Dr. John C. Horn, and the many Cub Scouters across the country who shared their ideas, photographs, and insights into those early years.

Thanks also to the current members of the national Cub Scout Committee and the countless other volunteers working on various national task forces who supported this project, including those volunteers who previewed the book and gave us additional insight. This book would not have been possible without their work. Specific thanks are extended to those who gave countless hours to help create this book:

The National Cub Scout Committee

Diane Cannon, Vice-Chairman
Mary Anne Rounds, Cub Scouting History Project Chairman
Cub Scouting History Task Force members Sue Hauser, Burts Kennedy, William Kuryla, William Stewart, and Tommy Thomas

Lyle R. Knight
Chairman
Cub Scout Committee

Alan Westberg
Director
Cub Scout Division

Part A: The Story

Chapter 1

THE BEGINNING: THE BSA'S YOUNGER BOY QUESTION

It was 1910. The Boy Scouts of America was just beginning. Boy Scout troops were sprouting almost spontaneously in cities and towns everywhere with little specific guidance.

James Edward West, a 34-year-old attorney, had just begun work as executive secretary of the BSA. One day a young Lyman Barry, resplendent in a Scout uniform, came into the office with his mother. West, who was to prove himself an organizational genius and zealous guardian of Scouting for more than 32 years as Chief Scout Executive, eyed the boy suspiciously.

James E. West

"How old are you, son?" he asked.

"Nine, sir."

"Then what are you doing in that uniform? Scouts must be at least 12."

The lad pointed out that the first *Boy Scout Handbook* of the movement, published in 1910, said 9-year-olds could join in "special cases." What the special cases were was not explained, so hundreds of younger boys were already in Scout troops.

When the boy and his mother left, West vowed this would never happen again. And so, on April 1, 1911, the BSA's National Executive Board adopted, at West's urging, a firm policy that boys must be at least 12 years old to join the Scouting movement.

No attempt was made to expel those younger boys who already were in troops; expulsions would have been impossible, in any case, because at the time Boy Scouts were not required to register so the national office had no records. In establishing the minimum-age policy, the National Executive Board also reached a consensus that careful planning should be undertaken to develop an organization for younger boys.

This was the first, but by no means the last, official mention of what came to be known as the "younger boy problem." For the next 19 years, the BSA's leaders wrestled with the idea of a program for younger boys. During much of that time, various youth programs thrived elsewhere in the world and in the United States.

"Junior Scouts" and British Wolf Cubbing

America's younger boys were not to be denied, with or without the approval of the Boy Scouts of America. In the two decades before the BSA adopted Cub Scouting in 1930, several Scouting-related programs for younger boys flourished throughout the United States.

In 1902, Ernest Thompson Seton, a famed author and illustrator, had begun the Woodcraft Indians for boys 12 to 15 years old. His program emphasized outdoor life and American Indian lore. By 1906, he had added a Little Lodge of Woodcraft Indians for boys and girls under the age of 12. Members could earn honors by passing tests in athletics, nature study, and outdoor living, and could reach successive ranks of Brownie, Woodman, Waterbearer, and Fire Keeper. Little Lodge "tribes" were divided into bands of six to 10 members. Each tribe had an elected chief and an adult head guide.

Robert S. S. Baden-Powell

The first Cub Scouts were called simply "Cubs," and their adult leaders were "Cubbers." In those days, a "Cub Scout" was a Boy Scout who had been a Cub.

While in England in 1906, Seton visited Robert S. S. Baden-Powell while B-P was still working out his ideas for what would become the Boy Scout movement in England. The two men exchanged information, and Seton later wrote that Baden-Powell had incorporated into Boy Scouting parts of the Woodcraft Indians program. Baden-Powell later publicly credited Seton as one of the fathers of Boy Scouting. Seton also would make vital contributions to the development of Cub Scouting in America.

The Boy Scout movement really began in 1907 in England with the publication of Baden-Powell's *Scouting for Boys.* British boys seized on the idea, and within weeks many troops formed there. After a few months, the Scouting idea had spread to other countries and to the United States. In 1909 there were Boy Scout troops (still unofficial) in Chicago, Illinois; Springfield, Massachusetts; Utica, New York; Paterson, New Jersey; several towns in Michigan; Sedalia, Missouri; Pawhuska, Oklahoma; and Salina, Kansas, among other cities. In both England and the United States, many early troops had "junior troops" or "cadet corps" of boys younger than 12. By 1911, "junior troops" in the United States had members as young as 9. Boys and parents were demanding the BSA establish a separate program for the hordes of younger boys.

That year, the National Executive Board asked Seton, the Chief Scout and one of the founders of the Boy Scouts of America, to formulate an outline for such a program. He immediately produced a workable plan called "Cubs of America," with a bear cub as the symbol. Boys would be organized in "Cub rings" with a "Cub mother," and the motto would be "We do our best"—just a hair's breadth from the motto adopted in 1930, "Do Your Best."

Unfortunately, at that time came a tremendous upheaval in the BSA as prominent men in the organization disagreed on vital issues, and the "younger boy program" again became a "problem." Seton's plans were shelved.

Meanwhile, in England, Baden-Powell also had been badgered since 1909 to do something for the young boys and had given his blessing to junior troops and patrols of "junior Scouts" within regular troops. A special program for younger boys gradually evolved. Baden-Powell cleverly drew its symbols and stories from *The Jungle Book,* written in Vermont in 1894 by his friend Rudyard Kipling, a commissioner in the British Scouting program. In 1916 Wolf Cubbing became an official part of British Scouting with the publication of *The Wolf Cub's Handbook.*

Wolf Cubs could earn the ranks of Tenderpad, One-Star Cub, and Two-Star Cub. Sometimes they camped out as guests of their closely affiliated Boy Scout troop.

Wolf Cubbing made rapid strides in England and elsewhere. By 1922, there were 104,000 Cubs in Great Britain and 20,000 others throughout Europe, Japan, Argentina, Australia, and Brazil, as well as an unknown (and officially unrecognized) number in the United States.

That book quickly made its way across the Atlantic and was the guide for many early Wolf Cub packs in Canada and the United States. Packs soon were using it in Detroit, Chicago, Seattle, Houston, Baltimore, Norfolk, and several Massachusetts communities. These packs followed the British plan of organizing by "sixes" (equivalent to today's dens) headed by a "sixer" (similar to our denner). Several sixes made up a pack led by a Cubmaster (Akela), who could be a man or a woman.

Wolf Cub Packs Stateside

By 1918, a Wolf Cub pack had formed in Butte, Montana, and two years later Paris, Texas, had a pack that boasted about 100 boys. That summer *The Paris Morning News* reported: "The boys are given hikes under careful direction and are also trained in loyalty, obedience, and service as the Scouts are. He is taught to be manly, not to cry when he stubs his toe or for minor injuries, is taught to take care of hurts and why they must be cared for, is taught loyalty to his country, flag, state, home, and school, to take care of his body, and many other things."

About the same time, Wolf Cubbing thrived in Stamford, Connecticut, too. The local council purchased badges and literature from Canada and welcomed Wolf Cubs to its summer camp. About a third of the campers in the summer of 1920 were Cubs. Harold G. Dye, who was assistant camp director, remembered, "I found (them) very eager to learn and quite capable of mastering many of the ideas of Scouting."

Two years later Dye started a Wolf Cub pack as an auxiliary of Boy Scout Troop 19 in the Brighton Presbyterian Church in Rochester, New York. "As we had in Stamford, Connecticut," he said, "I allowed the Cubs to go with the troop to summer camp in the summer of 1923 and each year after that while I was there." By the mid-1920s, Cubs were spending a week in camp during the summer in Ithaca, New York, too.

Individuals, not local councils, started most of the early Wolf Cub packs, and the boys did not go to camp. Among these packs was one formed in 1921 in the Congregational Church in Bristol, Connecticut. A member, Douglas Beals, remembered the leader was the church's youth director, an English lady named Pauline Chaulker.

"We had regular weekly meetings," Beals said. "There was a certain amount of training in the social arts—being a nice guy, learning to be polite, and so forth—as part of being a Wolf Cub. We were into such things as craft work, which didn't interest me much. But there was a lot of outdoor stuff which did interest me. We went on a lot of hikes, she being the typical English lady who tramps the moors and glens, and she'd be with us with her walking staff, helping the boys along."

At the other end of the nation, Wolf Cubbing began flourishing in Seattle in 1923 through the efforts of a transplanted Englishman, Sol G. Levy. At his urging, the Seattle Rotary Club sponsored a pack, which had 54 Wolf Cubs by 1928. The Chief Seattle Council even built a Cub camp called Camp Meaney adjacent to the Scout camp. James E. West was not happy about this and other Wolf Cub programs.

Keeping the Lid On

In those early years of Scouting in the United States, West absolutely opposed the idea of a program for young boys, for two reasons. First, he feared a second program would burden the movement with new problems while it was still in its adolescence. Second, he held the conviction that "the great need for boy work in America" was with boys 13 to 16 years old. "That is the time," he said, "when the home, the church, and other institutions have difficulty in holding them and making effective those values and influences which make for character building and citizenship training."

Later studies indicated the early years of a boy's life, 8 to 12, are vital ones for molding character and developing values.

Supporting West was another of the BSA's founders, Daniel Carter Beard, a noted author and editor and the national Scout commissioner. Beard apparently was influenced by anti-British sentiment in this country around the time of World War I and also by the term "Cubs," which he thought derogatory.

Daniel Carter Beard, first national Scout commissioner

But pressures continued to mount for a BSA program for younger boys. West kept them capped and controlled as best he could. He took the American copyright on the British *Wolf Cub's Handbook* in 1918, and for 10 years the National Supply Service sold this handbook to Cubmasters of Wolf Cub packs in the United States. It was West's way of keeping the lid on until the BSA was forced to create a younger boy program of its own. By the early 1920s, the pressure was intensifying.

In 1922, the Chief Scout Executive told professional Scouters the national office was keeping tabs on "experiments" with the programs for young boys. He also reported: "Our friends across the sea have been enthusiastic over the Wolf Cubs and have been concerned because we do not share that enthusiasm. We want to keep studying the subject and not be unmindful of our responsibilities to give leadership if something is actually needed."

In 1923, a questionnaire to the Scouting professionals in the field showed that a majority favored the adoption of a program for young boys. At a national conference in 1924, Scout executives extensively debated the "younger boy problem." By that time hundreds of Scout troops had "junior Scouts," "trailers," and "mascots."

In addition to these groups and the Wolf Cub packs, several other organizations, most quite small, offered boys under 12 a Scout-like program. The Piedmont Council in California had some 150 Boy Pioneers. They wore khaki shirts with red, gold, and silver ribbons on their sleeves denoting rank. For higher honors, Boy Pioneers could progress into two honor societies, the Mohawks and Mohegans.

Other councils had organized small groups of younger boys called American Eagles and American Eaglets. Later, in Jersey City, New Jersey, another small organization formed, called the American Tribesmen.

Probably the largest of the younger-boy programs with aims similar to Scouting was the Boy Rangers of America. This organization was the creation of Emerson Brooks, a retired business executive. He founded the first lodge of the Boy Rangers in Montclair, New Jersey, in 1913.

Boy Rangers "played Indian" and practiced pioneering skills. Their "Great Laws" copied the 12 points of the Scout Law. Their aim was to graduate into Boy Scouting, the Woodcraft Indians, or Boys' Clubs. At its peak in the mid-1920s, the Boy Rangers of America had 8,000 members and 700 lodges in 47 states.

With all of these small movements demonstrating the eagerness of younger boys for some form of organized activity leading to Boy Scouting, it was no surprise that at their 1924 national conference, Scout executives asked the National Executive Board "to proceed with such investigation as they deemed necessary, but to adopt some official program at as early a date as practicable."

Huber William Hurt, Ph.D., a psychologist and educator, did much of the research that led to the Cub Scout program.

Dr. Huber William Hurt

A graduate of Iowa Wesleyan University, Hurt received his doctorate from Columbia University. In 1911, he was an exchange professor in Germany. Later he was president of two colleges: Lombard College and McKendree College, both in Illinois. He was widely known as a lecturer as well as a researcher.

Hurt joined the Scouting movement in 1919, serving as Scoutmaster, Scout executive in Chicago, and national field commissioner, a roving professional Scouter who aided local councils. After helping to develop the Cub Scout program from 1927 to 1930, he was the first director of Cub Scouting, continuing in that post until 1934.

Subsequently, he worked on plans for programs for Senior Scouts and Air Scouting, a program for older Scouts that continued until 1965. He later became national director of research and of the reading program of the Boy Scouts of America. He was the author of 40 books, mostly on education.

Dr. Hurt retired from the BSA national staff in 1948 and died in Deland, Florida, on November 22, 1966.

Experiments in American Cubbing

The National Executive Board agreed on the need, and in 1925 the president of the BSA appointed a committee on the younger boy program. The chairman was William D. Murray, a lawyer and YMCA national official and a member of the BSA's National Council and Executive Board since its founding. Others on the committee were Professor Jeremiah Whipple Jenks of New York University, also an Executive Board member since 1910, and Dr. John Huston Finley, former college president and New York State Commissioner of Education who joined the board in 1921.

Dr. Huber William Hurt, a veteran Scouter, educator, and editor of the *Boy Scout Handbook for Boys* and *Handbook for Scoutmasters,* was appointed to make a study of existing organizations for younger boys. Extensive research found that only one boy in 50 was exposed regularly to a constructive leisure-time program. The study covered 30 agencies in the United States, Canada, and Europe enrolling younger boys, ranging from the YMCA and Boys' Clubs, through such church groups as the Catholic Boys' Brigade and Junior Christian Endeavor, to the Boy Rangers and British Wolf Cubs.

> The new American Cubbing program tried to steer clear of junior Boy Scouting. It was designed to focus on the home and neighborhood and provide things for boys to do between Cub meetings.

Dr. Hurt visited and worked closely with Ernest Thompson Seton, who devoted much time and effort to this project that had held his interest since 1911. Both men recommended the BSA adopt a program for younger boys, with older Scouts as leaders, to tie into home, church, school, and Boy Scouting.

More input came from E. S. Martin, secretary of the BSA's Editorial Board, who had visited Europe in 1925, talked with Wolf Cub leaders, and watched packs in action. In his report, which went to Scout executives in 1926, he recommended a program to be called "The Cubs." He proposed that the British Wolf Cub plan of organization by sixes and packs be used, that "junior Scouting" activities be avoided, and that Indian lore and pioneer life be emphasized.

Chief Scout Executive West gave cautious support to these suggestions. He had been helping Emerson Brooks incorporate the Boy Ranger program for possible adoption by the BSA, if forced to action. To his Scout executives he said the Executive Board probably would approve a program for younger boys "in those communities where it is needed." But, he emphasized, the new program must not jeopardize Boy Scouting, either by taking away funds or adult leaders or by encroaching on Scouting's program.

There was, however, no headlong rush to get a program going. Most BSA leaders believed the British Wolf Cub program was unsuitable for transplant to the United States, and objections were raised to the programs of the Boy Rangers and other groups.

Finally, in 1927, with a small share of a $50,000 grant from the Laura Spelman Rockefeller Foundation, Dr. Hurt began a thorough study that would lead to the development of American Cub Scouting. He and his secretary, C. Walter Seamans, worked with Ernest Thompson Seton in researching the characteristics of 9- to 12-year-old boys, how games and activities influence a boy's character, and how to adapt a program to a home and neighborhood setting. They went on the road to visit existing Wolf Cub packs and other groups for young boys in St. Louis; Seattle; Tulsa; Derby, Connecticut; and Seton's Woodcraft Indians Little Lodge in Cos Cob, Connecticut.

Dr. Hurt received further support in 1928 from the National Executive Board when an advisory committee of 22 noted educators was named to help analyze his studies and recommendations. Among the committee's members were philosopher and educator John Dewey and philosopher Dr. Elbert Kitlay Fretwell, dean of Columbia University's Teacher's College, who, in 1943, would succeed James E. West as Chief Scout Executive.

Elbert K. Fretwell

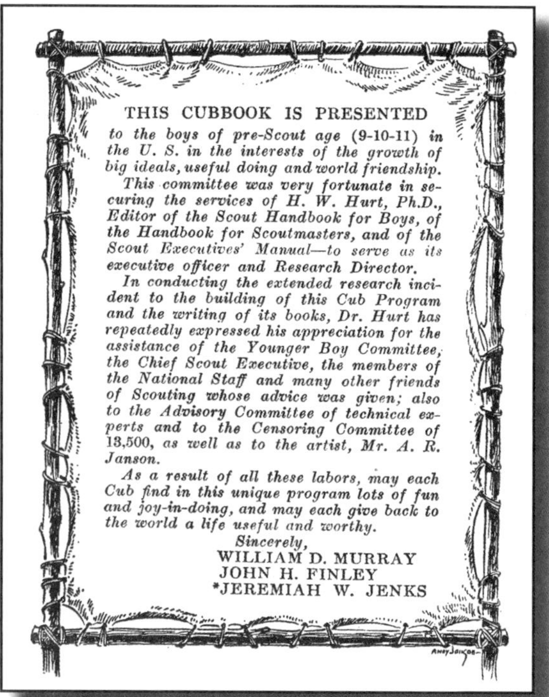

THIS CUBBOOK IS PRESENTED

to the boys of pre-Scout age (9-10-11) in the U. S. in the interests of the growth of big ideals, useful doing and world friendship.

This committee was very fortunate in securing the services of H. W. Hurt, Ph.D., Editor of the Scout Handbook for Boys, of the Handbook for Scoutmasters, and of the Scout Executives' Manual—to serve as its executive officer and Research Director.

In conducting the extended research incident to the building of this Cub Program and the writing of its books, Dr. Hurt has repeatedly expressed his appreciation for the assistance of the Younger Boy Committee, the Chief Scout Executive, the members of the National Staff and many other friends of Scouting whose advice was given; also to the Advisory Committee of technical experts and to the Censoring Committee of 13,500, as well as to the artist, Mr. A. R. Janson.

As a result of all these labors, may each Cub find in this unique program lots of fun and joy-in-doing, and may each give back to the world a life useful and worthy.

Sincerely,

WILLIAM D. MURRAY
JOHN H. FINLEY
*JEREMIAH W. JENKS

Presentation page from *The Boy's Cubbook,* Part 1—Wolf Rank, 1930

Some of Dr. Hurt's findings were field-tested in 1928 in experimental Cubbing units in each of the BSA's regions in 106 locations. By August 1929, the new Cubbing program (it was not officially called Cub Scouting until 1945) was taking shape and "demonstration units" were authorized. The first piece of Cubbing literature, *The Boy's Cubbook, Part I—Wolf Rank,* was sent to the printer in December 1929.

At the same time, the new program was being evaluated by 13,500 psychologists, educators, recreation and welfare leaders, and Scoutmasters. Most of them were Scoutmasters, many of whom doubled as Cubmasters for the demonstration packs.

In laying out the new program, Dr. Hurt and his secretary, Seamans, worked with Seton in adapting activities, games, and ceremonies they had seen while visiting American youth groups. They borrowed liberally from the Woodcraft Indians, Wolf Cubs, and the Boy Rangers of America. Seton stressed American Indian lore in place of *The Jungle Book* emphasis of Baden-Powell's Wolf Cubs.

In our first handbooks, "Akela" became an American Indian boy, son of the chief of the Webelos Tribe. *Webelos* was explained as a "word with an inner meaning, signifying progress from *W*olf through *B*ear and *L*ion ranks to *S*cout: W–B–L–S . . . We'll Be Loyal Scouts."

The chief of the Webelos Tribe was called "Arrow of Light," a name adapted from the Arrow Park World Jamboree in London in 1929 when the "Golden Arrow" was made the symbol of world friendship. According

Much of Ernest Thompson Seton's American Indian lore is found in Cub Scouting, yet all through the years the Cub Scouting story retained some of the flavor of Kipling's *The Jungle Book*. Such terms as Wolf, Bear, Bobcat, Tiger, den, pack, Akela, grand howl, Cub sign, etc., were adopted. Dr. Hurt recalled: "I deliberately recommended some things to tie in with the British," including the name "Akela" for a leader and Wolf as the first Cub rank. "Wolf, Bear, and Lion seemed a natural sequence," Hurt said. "The lion was a courtesy to the British lion." In later years, the name "Akela" was used for the chief of the tribe or pack. By 1980 a parent, an older brother or sister, or an adult friend could be Akela and help the Cub Scout along the advancement trail.

to *The Boy's Cubbook, Part I—Wolf Rank:* "The Arrow of Light has seven rays depicting the seven days of the week and a reminder to 'do one's best' every day. The Arrow forever points upward and onward toward good citizenship, and also has the meaning of world friendship symbolized by the Golden Arrow."

The Cubbing story told of the boy Akela being taken on trips into the forest, where, from the Wolf, he learned the language of the ground, the tracks, and ways to food; and how to care for himself. Then, as the boy grew older, the Bear taught him the secret names of trees and the calls of birds, how to live with others, and the weather signs—the language of the air. But, before the boy could become a Scouting "brave" on his own, he first had to look the Lion in the eye and learn the language of the stout heart—to fear nothing and never give up. Then, and only then, was the boy admitted to the lower ranks of the young "braves," the Scouts of the trail, advancing (at age 12) from the world brotherhood of Cubs into the world brotherhood of Scouts.

Seton Museum at Philmont

The tepees at Seton Village, Santa Fe, New Mexico, in 1980.

Ernest Thompson Seton was a famous wildlife artist, author, and lecturer before the turn of the 20th century. In 1902, Seton started an outdoor program for boys called the Woodcraft Indians. In 1910 he became a founder of the new Boy Scout movement and ranked among Scouting's best-known promoters in this country.

Ernest Thompson Seton

Seton's direct ties with the Boy Scouts of America ended in 1915 following disagreements with Chief Scout Executive James E. West. But his antipathy for West did not keep him from contributing to the Cub Scout program during the late 1920s.

Seton assisted Dr. Huber William Hurt in developing the program and gladly demonstrated his Woodcraft Indians methods at the camp on his estate in Connecticut. The American Indian emphasis in Cub Scouting in the early years can be traced to Seton's Woodcraft Indians.

In 1926, Seton received the seventh Silver Buffalo awarded by the Boy Scouts of America for national service to boyhood. He died in Sante Fe, New Mexico, in 1946. The BSA maintains a library and museum in his honor at Philmont Scout Ranch near Cimarron, New Mexico.

Chapter 2

THE 1930S:
CUB SCOUTING'S EARLY YEARS

The United States was sinking into the Great Depression in April 1930 when the Boy Scouts of America launched its Cub program for boys 9 through 11 years old. It was a gloomy time for the nation, but not for its youth.

The BSA was 20 years old and solidly established as the preeminent, and steadily growing, organization for older boys and young men. Membership stood at more than 600,000 Boy Scouts led by 200,000 adults in that first year of the Depression in the United States. With the coming of Cubbing, Boy Scouts could now hope to be free of their younger brothers, who had tagged along on troop activities and disturbed Scoutmasters for two decades.

Cub Scouters who remember those early days do so with pleasure. "It was great to be in Cubbing!" said Edmund D. Strang, a leader in Pack 3, Derby, Connecticut, when it obtained a charter in July 1930. Actually, Ed Strang had been a Cubber even longer. He had started an informal pack of the young hangers-on in his Boy Scout troop when he was a 17-year-old patrol leader in 1927. A year or so later, he heard about British Wolf Cubbing and began using that program.

When the BSA began its Cub program, his boys were ready. "The kids were so excited because here was a chance to get an official Cub Scout uniform, and kids were uniform-conscious in those days," he said. Although Strang was originally registered as assistant Cubmaster in 1930, he ran the pack from its start and continued in that role for more than 50 years.

> Training courses for new leaders were held that first year (1930) in eight of the BSA's 12 regions.

In St. Louis, the picture was much the same. In a *Scouting* magazine interview in 1980, Sam Reaves, the first Cub Scouting director in the St. Louis Area Council, remembered the enthusiasm of Cub-age boys and their parents when the council began experimental packs in 1929. "The boys were full of fire and enjoying it immensely," he said. "The moms and dads were so anxious for their boys to be a part."

The Cub program got off to a modest start in 1930. Between April and December, 243 packs obtained charters in 93 local councils. By the end of the year, 5,102 boys had become Cubs, and 1,433 adults were pack leaders.

In 1930 *The Boy's Cubbook, Part I—Wolf Rank* was published. Issued soon after were the Bear and Lion books, a *Parents' Cub Book,* and a *Cub Leader's Outline.*

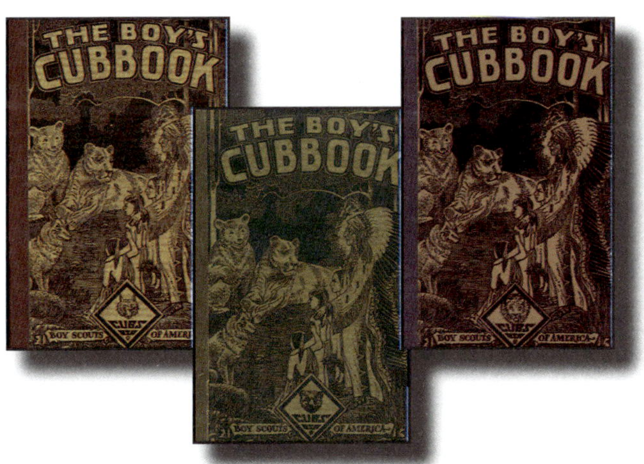

The national Committee on Cubbing kept a tight rein on the new program, making sure local councils had adequate human and financial resources before they plunged into Cubbing. A particular concern was that the new program might siphon off adult leaders from Boy Scouting. The committee was gratified to learn at the end of the first year that 76 percent of Cubbing's adult leaders were new to Scouting; only 24 percent of them came from Boy Scouting.

In the 1930s, Cubbing's organizational structure was like today's Cub Scouting except dens were led by Boy Scouts who were called den chiefs. The plan included a mothers' neighborhood committee to "encourage" Cubs and den chiefs, but there were no den mothers to lead dens. Then, as now, dens were to meet weekly at a member's home for games, ceremonies, and crafts. The pack was to meet weekly or semimonthly for games, den competitions, advancement awards, stunts, and other activities. The original program called for all Cubs to complete two Bobcat requirements, then advance to Wolf rank (for 9-year-olds), Bear (for 10-year-olds), and Lion (for 11-year-olds).

The National Council's careful control of Cubbing continued for three years. It was not until May 25, 1933, that the National Executive Board removed the "experimental" label and declared the program should be promoted aggressively. By that time, Cubbing had 34,000 boys and 4,600 leaders, and packs operated in more than 300 of the BSA's 550 local councils. By 1936, 10 percent of all boys registered in Scouting were in the Cub program. By the end of the year Cubbing had 70,880 boys and 11,704 pack leaders.

Cub Scout Den Leadership

Cubbing at the pack level was not much different in those early years from today's Cub Scouting. In the specifics, though, were significant differences.

The most important divergence was in the leadership of the basic unit, the den. As conceived by Dr. Hurt, who helped Ernest Thompson Seton write the first books, the den was to be led by a Boy Scout called the den chief. In theory, at least, there was no adult leader.

Reality was different, according to the recollections of leaders of early packs. Even then, the mother, in whose home the den meeting often was held, often functioned as a den mother, particularly when the den chief was not mature enough to deal with 9- through 11-year-old boys. But it was not until 1932 with the publication of the first *Cubmaster's Packbook* and *Den Chief's Denbook* that the den mother was recognized as part of the leadership team, although she was to "share" responsibilities with the den chief, not take charge. On paper, she was merely the liaison between the den and the neighborhood parents' committee.

By mid-1937, there were 659 registered den mothers, and they were being offered a uniform smock for $3.50. The smock was blue with gold piping and official Cub buttons. In 1938 a den mother's badge was approved.

Dens met weekly, as they do now, usually in a home. Den meetings were unstructured except for the opening and closing ceremonies—often the Cub Scout Promise, Law of the Pack, Living Circle, or grand howl, all of which survive today. In the early days, the heart of den meetings consisted of handicrafts, games, work on advancement requirements, and preparation of a skit, stunt, or special project for a pack meeting.

By the mid-1930s, it was clear that dens with adult leaders functioned better than those with only den chiefs. So on April 30, 1936, the BSA's National Executive Board approved optional registration of den mothers. (They were not required to register until 1948.) In the first *Den Mother's Denbook,* March 1937, the den mother was advised to "keep somewhat in the background, making the den chief the important figure in the den meeting."

Despite her secondary role, the den mother was told she needed to be "emotionally well balanced, have achieved some self-control, and happy adjustment for one's self. The den mother needs to have (1) an even temper; (2) a kindly (and not too distant) friendliness; (3) a quick buoyant smile; (4) a sense of humor, especially if the joke was on her—which is expected at times; (5) much patience and hope; (6) a recognition that normal boys are increasingly different from normal girls and probably less quiet and more active; (7) tact in dealing with people—old and young; and (8) ability to put one's self in the other's shoes."

Den mother uniforms

Cub Scouts having fun—important then, important now.

Monthly Pack Meetings

At first, packs met weekly in the afternoon for games, songs, stunts, story telling, and recognition ceremonies for advancement. In 1932, semimonthly pack meetings were being recommended. One meeting was to be an afternoon of outdoor fun for the boys only. The second was an evening meeting for parents as well as boys.

In most respects, this evening meeting was quite similar to today's monthly pack meeting, with songs, skits, recognition, and ceremonies. But there were two differences. Because monthly themes were not widely used, the activities had no unifying pattern. And because it was deemed vital to involve parents, the boys went off with their den chiefs to play games for part of the meeting while the parents met with the pack's adult leaders to discuss coming events, Cub advancement, and den and pack problems.

The practice of having separate sessions for parents at each pack meeting was not recommended until 1967. Later, separate meetings were held only in September when parents of new Cub Scouts were introduced to the program.

When Cubbing began, pack committee members and Cubmasters were all male, as far as official records were concerned. In fact, early Cubmasters often were women, and in 1931 the National Executive Board debated whether to register them. The first *Cubmaster's Packbook* made it clear only men could register as pack leaders. Dr. Hurt's secretary, Walter Seamans, explained that the rationale for this was American Indian tradition, the basis for the family program. Only males held prominent positions in some Indian tribes—examples for the young future leaders of the tribe.

Cub Leaders' Round Table

In November 1933, after the National Executive Board had decided Cubbing was here to stay, the BSA began publishing a monthly pamphlet called the *Cub Leaders' Round Table,* which offered registered leaders a medium for exchanging ideas for games, songs, skits, and ceremonies. Dr. Hurt was the editor. The first edition, Volume 1, Number 1, had greetings from James E. West and four pages from the national Cubbing committee.

Because den mothers could not be registered, they did not receive the *Cub Leaders' Round Table,* but hundreds read their husbands' copies and contributed ideas. By the late 1930s, den mothers were receiving the *Cub Leaders' Round Table,* too.

By the middle of the decade, more literature supporting den operation was being developed. In 1937, the Pack Financial Record Book was developed and the Pack Thrift Plan introduced. The *How Book of Cubbing* appeared in 1938. This book gave leaders program ideas in a variety of areas, including crafts, songs, games, and ceremonies.

Eager Cub Scouts test their Cubmobile in preparation for a pack Cubmobile race.

In April 1937, den leaders were given directions for making Cubmobiles, apparently the first vehicle for the various derbies that would become an annual feature of Cub Scouting. A Cubmobile was described as any contrivance on wheels (one, two, three, four, or more). In fact, most early Cubmobiles were patterned after Soapbox Derby racers. For several years, the Cub Leaders' Round Table showed photos and drawings of Cubmobiles, some very crude, foot-steered vehicles, and others worthy of Detroit's engineers.

Monthly themes, which point den activities in a single direction, did not come into vogue until 1940, though the Cub Leaders' Round Table included suggested themes. From 1934 to 1948, the Round Table introduced monthly program ideas. Scouting, the whole Scouting family magazine, contained the Cub Scout Program Helps in a special section in September of each year.

Early Leader Training

As early as 1933, the St. Louis Council offered an eight-week course (one session per week) for den mothers. In 1934, a national outline for Cub leader training was offered, and the Schiff Scout Reservation in Mendham, New Jersey, hosted national Cubbing courses three times that year. The next year brought a proposed training plan for Cubbing, including two 12-hour courses on activities leading to—after five years of experience—a proposed Cubmaster's Key or Cubber's Training Award, depending on the leader's position in the pack.

By 1939, some BSA local councils were holding annual gatherings of pack leaders in the council or its districts to encourage idea-swapping among leaders; show games, handicrafts, stunts, and skits; and give training in pack administration. By the end of the decade some councils were holding monthly roundtables, and the first pow wows were held, though official publications and support for these events did not come until much later. ("Pow wows" were first mentioned in the *Cubmaster's Packbook* in 1950 and in the *Den Mother's Denbook* a year later, but they apparently had been common in many councils for more than a decade.)

The Cub Scout leader's byword, "KISMIF," first appeared as a slogan for pow wows in 1939. KISMIF meant "Keep It Simple, Make It Fun," or "Keep It Short, Make It Fun."

Inspiration for KISMIF may have been an article in the *Cub Leaders' Round Table* in February 1938. Mrs. Charles Gustke, den mother of Pack 19 of Battle Creek, Michigan, wrote that she was amazed at the elaborate planning that went into some den meetings. Mrs. Gustke concluded: "The more simple and natural you can keep the den meeting the more the boys and you will enjoy it. The boys will feel more at home if it is very casual, and the mother will not feel that it has been too great an effort to have den meetings. Again, my plea is—keep them as simple and natural as possible."

Cub Scout Dinners

The blue and gold banquet, which today is the biggest annual event on the calendar of most packs, also was born during this period. Parent-Cub dinners were being suggested as early as 1933 in the *Cub Leaders' Round Table.* The following year in the Milwaukee Council the mothers of a pack prepared a father-son banquet, and a "fellowship banquet" was scheduled in Willcox, Arizona.

In 1935, Cub Pack 1 of Michigan City, Indiana, held a potluck dinner for Cubs and their parents. It took a good deal of preparation, not only by mothers, but also by the boys and their dads, because the invitation read: "The Cub's dad is requested to bring knives, forks, and spoons for himself and Cub. THESE UTENSILS MUST BE MADE OF WOOD AND CARVED, SAWED OR WHITTLED BY THE CUB AND HIS DAD! . . . Dads and Cubs must use the wooden utensils they have made. Everyone must be present. No excuses will be accepted."

The next several years produced occasional reports of father-and-son bean dinners and Cub family dinners. By the early 1940s, some packs were calling their annual dinner the "blue and gold banquet," and in 1943 the name began cropping up in Cub Scouting literature. For two or three years before that, planning for potluck or blue and gold dinners had been part of pow wow training.

Cub Uniforms

The Cub's first uniform was blue trimmed in gold but cut in a 1930s' style. The shirt was a pocketless, slipover jersey sweater or a two-pocketed dress shirt. The neckerchief was gold bordered in blue. For pants, boys could choose knickers or shorts, with knee-length blue stockings that had two gold stripes near the top. (The stockings weren't abandoned until 1947 when long trousers replaced the knickers.) The cap was described as a "college" cap with gold braid. Centered on its front was the BSA Cubbing emblem.

The official uniform of the 1930s—the Cubs on the right wear the official shirt, the ones on the left prefer the jersey. The full Cub uniform cost $6.05 in 1930, including shirt, pants, belt, neckerchief slide, socks, and cap.

Early Symbolism

The *Boy's Cubbook* for Wolf rank was published while the first packs were obtaining charters in April 1930. The book was quickly revised to change the Cub salute. In the original edition, the salute was the Indian sign for peace, with right arm upraised, palm out. Apparently leaders saw that the salute was disconcertingly similar to the Nazi salute of Adolf Hitler, who was beginning his rise to power in Germany en route to engulfing the world in war. The new salute became the familiar two-fingered touch of the right hand to the forehead.

The Cub sign, made with the right hand held high and straight above the shoulder, represented the alert ears of an animal. In American Indian sign language, it meant "intelligence" or "mental sharpness." The two spread fingers of the sign also referred to two points of the Cub Promise—to be square and to be loyal to family, home, and God; or (as various issues of the early books also say) to be square and to obey.

The Cub Promise in 1930 was written with just three lines:

I, (name), promise to do my best
to be square and
to obey the Law of the Cub Pack.

In later years, the Cub Scout Promise was changed twice, first to insert "to do my duty to God and my country" in 1950, and again in 1972 to change "to be square" to "to help other people."

Law of the Pack
The Cub follows Akela.
The Cub helps the pack go.
The pack helps the Cub grow.
The Cub gives good-will.

The Law of the Pack had several "secret meanings." In the early books, these secret meanings were written in code (backwards writing). In the Law of the Pack, the key words are *follows, helps,* and *gives.* The key letters are *F, H,* and *G.* One secret meaning is that the Cub is loyal to *f*atherland or country, loyal to *h*ome, and loyal to *G*od. A second secret meaning is that a Cub is *f*air, *h*appy, and *g*ame. These correspond to the three hidden fingers in the Cub sign. Some time later these three letters also came to mean family, home, and God.

Around the world, the Cub motto was Do Your Best.

The word *Webelos* also had a secret meaning. The 1930 books explained that "the Webelos tribal name has an inner meaning signifying progress from Wolf, through Bear and Lion ranks to Scout—W–b–l–s. The 'Arrow of Light' means progress upward and onward in that direction—the direction of good citizenship.

"W–B–L, the initials of the three ranks have a meaning abbreviated in the tribal name. We–be–lo–s. 'We'll be loyal' is that inner meaning. So the tribal name has an inner meaning of progress and of loyalty. That's what Cubs stand for."

The Living Circle has been an important part of Cub Scouting from the beginning.

The Living Circle symbolized that all Cubs are friends. The 1930 handbook explained that the Living Circle stands for five big ideals—one for each finger of the Cub's left hand, the hand used in the circle. These five ideals corresponded to the five fingers in the Cub sign: to be square, to be loyal, and (from the three hidden fingers) to be fair, happy, and game.

The Advancement Program

When a boy joined the Cub program, he had to pass the Bobcat requirements to earn the privilege of wearing the Cub uniform. The Bobcat requirements consisted of learning the Cub Promise and the Law of the Pack and getting his parents to agree in writing to help as members of the Cub Parent's Club.

By 1934 the Bobcat requirements had been changed to the following—more nearly like today's requirements:

1. Taken the Cub Promise
2. Explained and repeated the Law of the Pack
3. Explained the meanings of ranks
4. Shown the Cub Sign and Handclasp
5. Given the Cub Motto and the Cub salute

It was not until 1938 that a Bobcat pin was introduced to show that the boy had passed the Bobcat requirements. The pin was to be worn only on civilian clothes, not on the uniform.

After passing the Bobcat entrance tests, 9-year-old Cubs began work in the Wolf *Cubbook;* 10-year-olds in the Bear book; and 11-year-olds in the Lion book. With minor exceptions, the subject matter of achievements and electives was the same for all three ranks, but the degree of challenge increased with age.

For example, Achievement 1 for all ranks was called "The Flag." A 9-year-old working toward Wolf rank had to learn the Pledge of Allegiance, basic flag courtesies, and something about the national origins of his den's families. The 10-year-old trying for Bear rank learned some U.S. flag history and colored a map of the world showing countries that had Cubbing programs. The 11-year-old Lion aspirant had to demonstrate advanced flag courtesies, meet the Boy Scout Tenderfoot requirements concerning the U.S. flag, and show some knowledge of world geography or current events.

The other 11 achievements in all three ranks had similar gradations of skill based on age. After passing all 12 achievements to his den chief or Cubmaster (not to parents, as boys do today), the Cub received his new badge and began working on 24 electives to earn Arrow Points. Some of the original electives are familiar to today's Wolf and Bear Cub Scouts: Secret Codes, Handicrafts, Radio, Electricity, Model Boats, Aircraft, Things That Go, Indian Crafts, Drawing, Nature, Animals and Pets, Garden, Soils, and Bachelor Cooking.

The badges of rank originally were called the "Bronze" badges. After earning the badge of rank for his age, a Cub could work on "honor arrow points." A Gold Honor Arrow Point showed that the Cub had completed 10 extra honor point electives, and 10 beyond that for the Silver Honor Arrow Point. These were worn on the uniform in a similar manner as today, with the Gold Honor Arrow Point directly under the badge of rank, and Silver Honor Arrow Points under them.

Early Cubs wore only their current badge of rank and Arrow Points. The practice of wearing all earned badges began in 1941. The first Cubs were allowed to sew all of their Cub badges on their merit badge sashes when they became Boy Scouts.

Cubbing Comes Into Its Own

By 1935, American Cubbing was well established and growing briskly. At the end of that year, 57,000 boys and 9,500 adults were registered. In the national office came a changing of the guard as William C. Wessel took over from H. W. Hurt as director. C. Walter Seamans continued as assistant.

Some of the BSA's pioneer leaders still thought of Cubbing as a stepchild. For example, Cub membership records were lumped in with Boy Scouts in national statistics.

At a national Scout executives' conference in 1936, Wessel noted that on big charts showing national statistics, all totals that included Cubs were marked with an asterisk. Recruiting two sympathizers, he stealthily turned each asterisk into a big, bright daisy. One of the artists was Ray L. Weaver, former director of the BSA's Schiff Scout Reservation, who remembered: "This joke, plus the fact that Scout advancement and camping records suffered when Cubs were counted as Scouts, did the trick. Soon all national records showed the number of Cubs, numbers of packs, and so forth."

James E. West, Chief Scout Executive during the BSA's first 33 years, rejoiced as Cubbing prospered. He had been less than enthusiastic about starting a new program for younger boys, because he foresaw administrative nightmares for his overburdened office. But he was delighted with the reality of Cubbing's growth.

One concern of West and other top leaders had been that Cubbing might infringe upon Boy Scouting. This was by no means unlikely since many Scoutmasters served as early Cubmasters. The national office issued frequent admonitions, like this one in 1932:

- Do not even parallel Scouting.
- In operating Cubbing, keep as far away from Scouting as possible.
- Scouting is community-centered—Cubbing is home-centered.
- Scouting revolves around a meeting—Cubbing around between-meetings.
- Scouting has city-wide events—Cubbing has neighborhood events.

Cub Scouting's second director (but the first to hold that title) was William C. Wessel, who served from 1935 until his death in 1949.

Wessel was born in Brooklyn, New York, in 1893 and was educated at Syracuse University's New York College of Forestry. While in college he became interested in Scouting and took leadership training for a position as assistant Scoutmaster. He also was a local council instructor for nature study and forestry.

William C. Wessel

He entered professional Scouting in 1920. Fifteen years later Wessel was appointed director of Cub Scouting, succeeding Dr. Huber W. Hurt, who had guided the program through its infancy.

"We must keep Cubbing sharply and distinctly different from Scouting in order not to steal from or trespass upon Scouting. We must even be careful not to unconsciously imitate or parallel Scouting. Keep Cubbing different! Keep it home-centered!"

Some early leaders needed that advice because they did trespass on Boy Scouting. But by 1939, as Cub Scouting neared its 10th anniversary, it was quite separate and distinct from Boy Scouting. Membership was growing briskly with 159,637 boys and 28,213 adults enrolled at the end of that year.

Chapter 3

THE 1940S:
CUB SCOUTING COMES OF AGE

The decade of the 1940s was a fateful time for the United States. A united people emerged victorious after nearly four years of the cataclysm of World War II.

It also was a growing-up period for Cub Scouting. Along with their older brothers in Boy Scouting and Exploring, Cub Scouts on the home front contributed much to the war effort. Membership grew rapidly, and by the end of 1949 Cub Scouting had reached the million mark for the first time, a more than fivefold increase since the start of the decade.

The basic program was changing, too. In January 1940, the first monthly theme was offered to give Cubmasters and den mothers ideas for a coherent program. The ideas for themes came from Gerald A. Speedy, who took over as editor of the *Cub Leaders' Round Table* when he became assistant director of Cubbing. The lead article in the *Cub Leaders' Round Table* was titled "Theme, Theme, My Kingdom for a Theme!" The first recommended theme was "Be Kind to Birds."

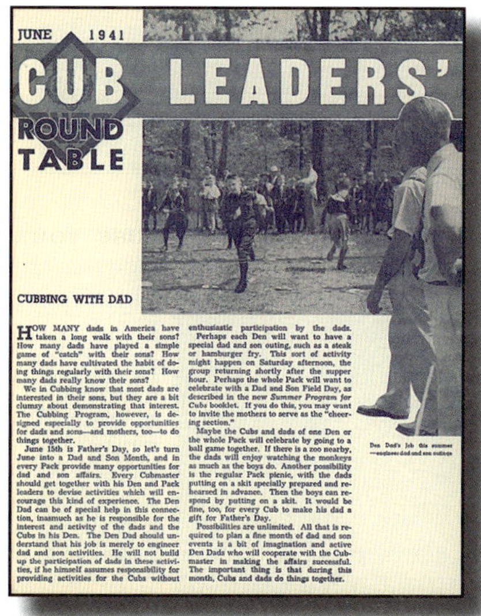
JUNE 1941

CUB LEADERS' ROUND TABLE

CUBBING WITH DAD

HOW MANY dads in America have taken a long walk with their sons? How many dads have played a simple game of "catch" with their sons? How many dads have cultivated the habit of doing things regularly with their sons? How many dads really know their sons?

We in Cubbing know that most dads are interested in their sons, but they are a bit clumsy about demonstrating that interest. The Cubbing Program, however, is designed especially to provide opportunities for dads and sons—and mothers, too—to do things together.

June 15th is Father's Day, so let's turn June into a Dad and Son Month, and in every Pack provide many opportunities for dad and son affairs. Every Cubmaster should get together with his Den and Pack leaders to devise activities which will encourage this kind of experience. The Den Dad can be of special help in this connection, inasmuch as he is responsible for the interest and activity of the dads and the Cubs in his Den. The Den Dad should understand that his job is merely to engineer dad and son activities. He will not build up the participation of dads in these activities, if he himself assumes responsibility for providing activities for the Cubs without enthusiastic participation by the dads.

Perhaps each Den will want to have a special dad and son outing, such as a steak or hamburger fry. This sort of activity might happen on Saturday afternoon, the group returning shortly after the supper hour. Perhaps the whole Pack will want to celebrate with a Dad and Son Field Day, as described in the new *Summer Program for Cubs* booklet. If you do this, you may want to invite the mothers to serve as the "cheering section."

Maybe the Cubs and dads of one Den or the whole Pack will celebrate by going to a ball game together. If there is a zoo nearby, the dads will enjoy watching the monkeys as much as the boys do. Another possibility is the regular Pack picnic, with the dads putting on a skit specially prepared and rehearsed in advance. Then the boys can respond by putting on a skit. It would be fine, too, for every Cub to make his dad a gift for Father's Day.

Possibilities are unlimited. All that is required to plan a fine month of dad and son events is a bit of imagination and active Den Dads who will cooperate with the Cubmaster in making the affairs successful. The important thing is that during this month, Cubs and dads do things together.

Den Dad's job this summer—engineer dad and son outings

Previously the *Cub Leaders' Round Table* booklet had offered helps for leaders mainly by printing "success stories" from Scout executives and others. Beginning in 1940, it began to recommend monthly themes and give supporting projects and suggestions for specific den and pack crafts, games, ceremonies, and other activities.

The year saw other important developments. William D. Murray, who had been national Cubbing chairman since before the program became official in 1930, died November 20, 1939. Industrialist John M. Bierer of Norvell, Massachusetts, succeeded Murray in 1940.

Also in 1940, the *Summer Program* pamphlet promoted Cubbing as a summertime activity. Pow wows became more common in local councils, and the first den chief training course was launched.

The third director of Cub Scouting, Gerald A. Speedy, was a native of Minneapolis, Minnesota, who joined the Scouting movement in 1922. He was familiar with various younger-boy programs that preceded Cub Scouting, and he served as a Cubmaster during Cubbing's early days.

Gerald A. Speedy

He began his professional Scouting career in 1935 as Cub Scout director of the Minneapolis Area Council. While serving there, he wrote the first Cub Scout activities book, the *How Book of Cubbing.* The book was originally a Region 10 project, and Chief Scout Executive James E. West reprimanded Regional Executive Kenneth Butz for producing Cubbing literature. In 1943, when West was retiring, Speedy remembered he ran into the Chief in the hall of the national office and said his farewells. As West walked off, he looked back and shouted, "Boy, see that you don't write any more bootleg literature!"

Speedy had joined the national staff as assistant director of Cubbing in 1940. Immediately, he established the monthly theme as the basis for pack programs. He also rewrote the early editions of the basic boys' books, the *Cubmaster's Packbook,* and the *Den Mother's Denbook.*

When Wessel died in 1949, Speedy succeeded him as director and served for three years. Then from 1952 to 1957, he was assistant director of the Program Division, and then later its director until his retirement.

The Advancement Program Changes

The next two years brought two major changes in the boys' advancement program. In 1941, the Webelos rank was created for the 11½ -year-old boy who had earned his Lion badge and completed several requirements toward the Tenderfoot rank in Boy Scouting.

In 1942, the requirement that a Cub must start with the Wolf rank, regardless of his age at joining, was eliminated. Previously a boy who joined Cubbing at 11 had to complete the Wolf and Bear achievements and earn those badges before he could start working on Lion, the natural rank for his age.

A boy who joined as a 10-year-old had two choices of where to begin the advancement program after he completed the Bobcat requirements. He could take a little extra time to complete the Wolf achievements and receive his Wolf badge before going ahead with the Bear achievements. Or, he could start on his Bear achievements as soon as he completed three "catch-up" requirements that showed he was ready to work on the Bear achievements. These catch-up requirements, which covered some essentials from the Wolf achievements, were to give the Pledge to the Flag of the U.S.A.; to explain the rules of street safety; and to tie shoestrings, a necktie, and a package.

By that time, Cubs were being permitted to wear on their uniform shirt all badges of rank and Arrow Points they had earned. In the early days, they had worn only the current badge of rank with its Arrow Points.

Cub Scouts Help War Effort

On December 7, 1941, Japanese planes attacking the American fleet at Pearl Harbor, Hawaii, plunged the United States into World War II. The next day, the Boy Scouts of America pledged its full resources of man and boy power to help the war effort.

Actually, the BSA's homefront work had begun even before the Pearl Harbor bombing. As part of the nation's preparedness campaign, Boy Scouts and Cub Scouts had already had nationwide newspaper and aluminum collection campaigns during the spring and summer of 1941.

But with the U.S. entry into the conflict, the BSA stepped up its services. No separate statistics were kept for Cub Scouts' participation in the BSA's wartime service, but there is little doubt Cub Scout packs participated in the same proportion to their numbers as did Boy Scout troops.

By the time World War II ended in August 1945, Boy Scouts and Cub Scouts had delivered millions of War Bond pledge cards. It was estimated they were indirectly responsible for selling $1.8 million worth of bonds and War Savings Stamps.

In periodic waste collection campaigns the federal government requested during the war, the BSA accounted for 5,898 tons of rubber, mostly old tires; 17,400 tons of tin cans; and 20,800 tons of other scrap metal. With few synthetic substitutes, recyclable rubber was essential for war production. The war had cut off the raw rubber supply from the Far East. All types of metal also were essential for wartime production. Other items collected for the war efforts were grease (used in the manufacture of munitions), newspapers (for recycling), and milkweed seeds and milkweed floss (used for fill in life jackets and for filters in gas masks).

The largest single project in the war years was the General Dwight D. Eisenhower Waste Paper campaign in the spring of 1945. More than 700,000 Boy Scouts and Cub Scouts collected 318,000 tons of paper, bringing the BSA's total paper collection during the war to 591,000 tons.

Victory gardens were popular projects. By 1944 an estimated 184,000 Cub Scouts and Boy Scouts had planted gardens to help ease the nation's food shortage. Gardening was a popular monthly theme.

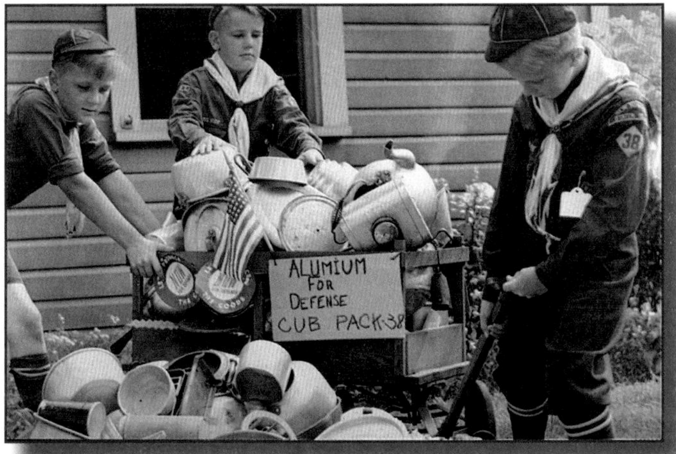

Cub Leaders' Round Table Provides Ideas

The *Cub Leaders' Round Table* was full of reports of war service undertaken by dens and packs. In the spring of 1942, for example, Den 1 of Pack 21, West Hartford, Connecticut, was shown making cartoon scrapbooks for U.S.O. clubs and U.S. Army and U.S. Navy posts. Pack 345 of Houston, Texas, made solid scale models of military aircraft to be used in pilot training. In Highland Park, New Jersey, Den 3 of Pack 2 converted cigar boxes into kits holding whistles, flashlights, notebooks, and other equipment for air-raid wardens.

In 1943 Pack 19, operated by Wilshire Post 319 of the American Legion in Los Angeles, received applications for more than $90,000 worth of War Bonds and Stamps. One of its Cub Scouts, Nat Jeffries, was raising and training carrier pigeons for military service.

Concern arose that Cubs might be called upon to tackle wartime service beyond their abilities. And so in the *Cub Leaders' Round Table,* September 1942 issue, leaders were advised to consider "all War Service projects with the total boy and man power in mind. Many projects can be planned so that Cubs and Scouts each assume their proper share, while other projects are beyond the scope of Cubs."

Specifically, Cubbers were told to keep projects home- and neighborhood-centered; to make sure they were not beyond the skills and strength of the Cub Scouts; and to plan projects that would enhance parental involvement, thereby strengthening the family.

The September 1944 *Cub Leaders' Round Table* made the following monthly report on war service by Cub Scouts:

Cub Pack 2 of Allston, Mass., has been doing war service work in its own special way. Under the guidance of the den mothers and other officers, and under the direction of Harold Embree, their Cubmaster, they have been sharing their Fifth Annual Minstrel Show, entitled "Victory Minstrels," with servicemen stationed near Allston. They have visited several camps and hospitals and have entertained countless men and women who wear the uniform of Uncle Sam.

Pack 9, located at the Punahou Elementary School in Honolulu, recently completed a project of making over 200 ash trays which were taken to American Red Cross Headquarters and, in turn, placed in numerous hospitals for our servicemen.

White Eagle Den, Cub Scouts of Pack 2, Salt Lake City, Utah, appeared at the U.S.O. one day—each with a gift for a crippled serviceman at Bushnell Hospital. The gift was a cane made from a mop or broom handle, polished and varnished, fitted with a nonskid rubber tip, and a padded grip so as not to hurt the user's hand when he leaned upon it. These canes were described in the January 1944 issue of the *Cub Leaders' Round Table*.

Still more about those popular "Kits for the Guys who have been Hit." Cub Scouts of Pack 78, Baltimore, Md., furnished 55 of these kits to the servicemen in Marine Hospital, Washington, D.C. Mr. Baxter is their Cubmaster.

Pack 24 of Oakland, Calif., recently completed and turned over to the Red Cross 150 weaving looms to be used by convalescent soldiers. This same pack joined in a drive to raise funds to purchase a Seeing-Eye dog for some returning soldier.

Pack 147, Hackettstown, N.J., has completed a large number of scrap books which have been sent to hospitalized soldiers. Their Cubmaster, J. A. McClary, suggests that if other packs undertake the project, they should give special emphasis to short stories, jokes, and pictures, because these are the things that Pack 147 has found most popular with servicemen. One soldier told the Cubmaster that magazines and books get worn out very quickly in a hospital. This particular soldier has been confined in a hospital ward for eleven months.

"Cubbing" Becomes Cub Scouting

Even while the war raged and Cub Scouts did their part for the nation, some fixtures of today's Cub Scouting were evolving, including a change in terminology. In 1945 the term "Cubbing" was dropped in favor of "Cub Scouting." Gerald Speedy remembered: "We had never been able to get people to use the term 'Cubbing,' so we decided to join them and make 'Cub Scouting' official. Strangely, after this was done we had difficulty getting people to call the program 'Cub Scouting.' Oh well! That's the way it was in the early time."

Speedy added: "In the time I have been describing, we tried to bring two major principles to bear on all we did. First, there was much emphasis on spirit. When the pow wow was developed, this was a major focus, as it was in all training materials. We knew that if the program was to work, it would do so only under a spirited leadership of professionals and volunteers. Second, we felt it necessary to create enough changes in the early years to guarantee against traditionalizing the program too soon. Looking back, I think both these points of emphasis were sound and necessary."

Beginning in 1948, all den mothers had to be registered. Registration by den mothers had been optional until this time.

Monthly Roundtables Begin

Monthly roundtables for Cub Scout leaders within a district began developing during the war years, too. Designed to provide inspiration and program ideas for the following month's theme, roundtables were first mentioned in the January 1941 issue of the *Cub Leaders' Round Table.* The story reported several councils already holding roundtables for their Cub Scout leaders. The Sequoia Area Council in Fresno, California, had been holding monthly roundtables for two years by then and boasted an average attendance of at least 100. The West Suburban Council at LaGrange, Illinois, and the Seattle Area Council also were holding monthly roundtables. In the Nassau County Council on Long Island, New York, councilwide roundtables drawing more than 100 leaders were being held three times a year.

Other councils with regular roundtables by that time were in Springfield, Massachusetts; East Orange, New Jersey; Wilmington, Delaware; Shreveport, Louisiana; Glendale, California; Roanoke, Virginia; Detroit, Michigan; and Atlanta, Georgia.

These early roundtables apparently were discussion forums rather than practice and demonstration of skills, although they sometimes featured craft exhibits.

***The Cubmaster's Packbook,* 1943**

In the 1943 edition of the *Cubmaster's Packbook,* the reader was told: "There are few formal presentations at district roundtables, but plenty of opportunity for discussion. Cubmasters who enjoy rubbing elbows with other Cubbers in small groups will cooperate with their commissioners who frequently act as leaders at such meetings on a district basis."

After the War

The postwar period brought additional changes to Cub Scouting. In 1947, long trousers became part of the official uniform. Cub Scouts could still wear knickers if they wanted to, but leaders were warned in the *Cub Leaders' Round Table* that knickers were no longer being manufactured. Boys of the era no longer wore knickers as part of their regular clothing.

The year 1949 brought a major change in Cub Scouting when the age levels for membership dropped by a year. Beginning in September, boys could join at 8 years of age and continue through their 10th year. The other programs—Boy Scouting and Exploring—also dropped their entry ages by a year, so that boys could join Boy Scouting at 11 and Exploring at 14.

The age changes came after a three-year study, including conferences with leading educators and pack, troop, and post leaders. One result was an immediate spurt in enrollment of boys in Cub Scouting.

Cub Scouting ended the 1940s with membership of 766,635 boys registered and 215,724 pack leaders—nearly five times the number enrolled at the beginning of the decade. Cub Scouting's enrollment still trailed Boy Scouting by a third, but it was closing fast.

Chapter 4

THE 1950S: TAKING OFF

Cub Scouting had grown briskly, even spectacularly, during its first 20 years. But with the baby boom that followed World War II, the program's growth was nothing short of phenomenal.

Millions of GIs rushed out of service, married, and started families. By the time their first sons were reaching Cub Scout age in the mid-1950s, Cub Scouting was recording gains of 200,000 new members a year.

The postwar period was a time of increasing affluence and rising living standards. Young families had more and better housing, more cars, more household appliances, and more leisure time than their parents did. Families were more child-centered, too, and for Cub Scouting that translated into deep parental involvement in the program. Compared with today, it was relatively easy to recruit den and pack leaders and to get parental help for special pack activities.

During the 1950s, the Cub Scout program was further refined. The basis of the Webelos den for 10-year-old Cub Scouts was put in place, and the activities in the advancement program for younger boys became more varied. New activities included the pinewood derby, now a highlight of the program year in many packs, and the first regattas for model boats. As they had in World War II, Cub Scouts joined their big brothers in Boy Scouting for several national Good Turns during the decade.

Explosive Growth Under Bud Bennett

Guiding Cub Scouting during most of the 1950s and through the 1960s was a dynamic leader named O. W. (Bud) Bennett. He became director of Cub Scouting in 1952 when Gerald Speedy moved up as assistant director of the BSA's Program Division. For the next 18 years, Bud Bennett was "Mr. Cub Scouting."

Bennett was a talented artist. His cartoons and illustrations soon adorned the pages of Cub Scouting literature. He also made a point of getting out into the field to see what was happening in Cub Scouting at the local level.

John C. Horn, a member of the national Cub Scout Committee during the last nine years of Bennett's service, remembered this about Bennett:

"When he became director, he saw the thousands of Cub Scout packs active in various parts of the nation as one vast but diversified laboratory where new ideas and programs could be developed and tested. Probably that was what

O. W. (Bud) Bennett, Cub Scouting's fourth director, would hold the longest tenure in that post, 18 years. He served from 1952 to 1970, during the period of Cub Scouting's fastest growth.

A native of Redfield, South Dakota, Bennett was a Boy Scout in his youth. He attended the University of Minneapolis and the Minneapolis Advertising and Display School. During 14 years in advertising and sales promotion work, he was a volunteer Scouter serving as assistant Scoutmaster and field commissioner for Cub Scouting.

Bennett entered professional Scouting in 1941, serving local councils in Toledo and Middletown, Ohio, before joining the national staff in 1947 as assistant to the director of Scouting Services. He had been director of Exploring for three years when he was named director of Cub Scouting in 1952.

The infectious nature of Bennett's personality permeated all his work as Cub Scouting's director. To those who came into Cub Scouting after his retirement, it is difficult to describe this special person. But his legacy remains. Today's Cub Scouting is bigger and better for his having been with us.

Bud Bennett retired as Cub Scouting director in 1970 and from professional Scouting soon after, although he continued to advise his successor, Robert L. Untch. Bennett died in Piscatawy, New Jersey, in 1974.

motivated him to say to his worthy assistant, Marlin Sieg, 'Let's drop things here at the office and see what's going on out there!' This started a series of visits that lasted until all parts of the country had been visited."

As Sieg recounted, "those were strenuous days but they paid off in knowledge and the direction of our program."

When Bennett arrived on the local scene, he made sure he was with pack leaders. His enthusiasm permeated these important people in Cub Scouting as he became their partner working at the local level on problems and opportunities right there at home. It is no wonder the friendship circle of Cub Scouting grew by leaps and bounds; once made, these friendships carried on for years to come.

The local scene was a rich source of ideas for Bennett. His constant self-inquiry was "How can we get these ideas across to others quickly and in a fun-type manner?" Here his artistic talents were put to work. He turned the ideas collected in his grassroots contacts into sketches for bulletins, leaflets, training filmstrips, posters, and *Scouting* magazine articles. His sketches confirmed concepts, demonstrated methods, or presented with great humor homely situations that pack leaders could use. Pack and den leaders could relate to them easily.

Bennett's able assistant, Marlin S. Sieg, joined the national staff of the Boy Scouts of America in 1949 as assistant director of Cub Scouting. Together with national chairmen Robert N. Gibson, named in 1954, and H. H. Coffield in 1959, they guided the burgeoning Cub Scout program through the period of explosive growth.

In a 27-year career as assistant director of the Cub Scout Division, Marlin S. Sieg left his imprint on the program. For many years he compiled and edited the *Cub Scout Program Quarterly* and later *Cub Scout Program Helps.* He also trained thousands of leaders in courses all over the country.

Sieg was a native of Red Wing, Minnesota. He became a Scout in 1925 and earned the Eagle Scout Award. After graduating from St. Olaf College, where he played football and was a member of the track team, he became a high school biology teacher and coach at Pipestone, Minnesota, for eight years.

He became a professional Scouter in 1941 and served in local councils at Wheeling, West Virginia, and Canton and Toledo, Ohio, before joining the national staff in 1949.

As assistant director of Cub Scouting until 1976, he was much involved in developing training plans as well as program. He did much of the pioneering work for pow wow and roundtable training plans, den chief conferences, and revisions of the basic Cub Scout leaders' training courses. Sieg continued to lead training courses for Cub Scouters after his retirement in 1976. He lived in Columbus, Georgia, and died in February 1986. He received the Silver Beaver Award for his volunteer efforts.

The Cub Scout Promise Changes

The Cub Scout Promise was changed in the 1950 printing of the handbooks, adding a new line—"to do my duty to God and my country." This line had always been part of the Scout Oath. The Promise now read:

I, (name), promise to do my best
To do my duty to God and my country,
To be square, and
To obey the Law of the Pack.

The Webelos Den Concept Is Born

Dave Hoover, the vice-chairman of the national Cub Scout Committee during most of Bennett's tenure as director, remembered the following:

> One of Bud Bennett's biggest assets was his relationship with the field. He was acquainted with Cub Scouters in every council across the nation, and it was a mutually advantageous friendship. One of the truisms which Bud knew and practiced was that there are more good programs 'out there' than he would ever have, and the challenge was to develop them where they were.
>
> My earliest encounter with Bud Bennett was in the fifties. I was a pack committee chairman, and the Cubmaster and I were talking about the 10-year-olds losing interest in the program. We decided to set up a special den for those Cub Scouts; the den would meet Friday nights, a time when their dads could be present.
>
> We named it Den 10 for the age of the Cub Scouts. Before we went much further, I called up a local resident who was on the national Cub Scout Committee. When I told him what we had in mind, he gave me more reasons why it could not be done than you could imagine. We went ahead anyway with marvelous results. Maybe this was the reason why I found myself being asked to join that August group, the national Cub Scout Committee. On this body, I found nothing but wholehearted support for the Webelos den concept, and the biggest supporter was Bud himself, who added his own ideas to it to make it an even better program.
>
> This is a perfect example of how the field was ahead of the committee, and also how Bud used the field to find answers for others. He was forever encouraging creativity among pack leaders. After all, they are the closest to the boy, and it is in the field that creative development is needed."

Development of the Webelos den idea followed a two-year study of the entire Cub Scout program during the early 1950s. Several changes also were made in the advancement plan for younger boys, but the most important departure was provision of the Webelos den for 10½-year-olds who had earned Lion rank. The changes became effective in the spring of 1954. A new handbook called the *Lion–Webelos Book* was published in 1954 for boys who had just turned 10 and for those in their last six months of Cub Scouting.

The design for the new Webelos den encouraged an easy transition of Cub Scouts into Boy Scouting. The leader was a man who registered as assistant Cubmaster. It was recommended that Webelos dens meet in the leader's home in the evening or on Saturday rather than after school, as was customary for regular Cub Scout dens.

> The boys in the Webelos den continued to be called "Cub Scouts." The change to "Webelos Scouts" came 13 years later, in 1967, when the Webelos program was thoroughly evaluated and redesigned.

The Advancement Plan Gets a New Look

The advancement plan for younger Cub Scouts changed in some respects, too. Previously all three ranks—Wolf, Bear, and Lion—had achievements and electives with the same titles and substantially the same requirements. The boy was challenged to do better work as he grew older.

With the changes introduced in 1954, the titles of achievements and electives varied for each rank, and so did some requirements. Under the new plan, the first achievement was "Feats of Skill" for Wolf; "Young Athlete" for Bear; and "Muscle Builders" for Lion. Requirements were written to challenge the natural development of the boy. Similarly, the first elective for each rank was varied: for Wolf Cub Scouts, it was "Secret Codes;" for Bear, "Indian Signs;" and for Lion, "Signals." The purpose was to satisfy the boy's broadening interests and to give him a progressive series of tests to pass as he grew through the Cub Scouting years.

1954 Editions of Wolf, Bear, and Lion books

To support the extensive revisions in the program, new editions of the books came out in 1954: *Wolf, Bear,* and *Lion–Webelos Cub Scout Books, Den Chief's Denbook,* and *Cubmaster's Pack Book.* Four years later, the leader of the Webelos den received additional help with the publication of the *Webelos Den Book,* which contained den meeting outlines.

If a boy became a Cub Scout at age 9, he had a choice to make after completing the Bobcat requirements. He could start on the Wolf achievements and receive his Wolf badge, or he could choose to start immediately on the Bear achievements, in which case he could not receive the Wolf badge. By 1958, the Bobcat pin (which was introduced in the late 1930s but not for wear on the uniform) could be worn on civilian clothes or the uniform shirt, but only until the Cub Scout had earned his first rank.

The Pinewood Derby Appears

In 1953 a Cubmaster discovered that his son and other 10-year-olds were too young to participate in the Soap Box Derby, so he created a simpler project that a younger boy could build with his father. On May 15, 1953, the first pinewood derby was run at the Scout House in Manhattan Beach, California, with 55 Cub Scouts from Pack 280C participating.

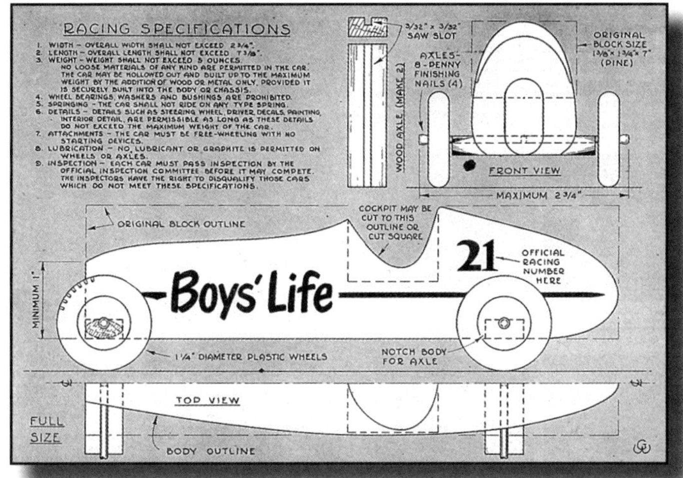

The pinewood derby first appeared in Scouting's publications in the October 1954 issue of *Boys' Life,* which told how to make one of the gravity-powered racing car models and the track to run it on. As early as 1939, the BSA's Supply Division had listed kits for model trains, boats, and airplanes, but this was the first appearance of the racing car built since by millions of boys and parents.

In 2003, 50 years later, more than 1.4 million pinewood derby cars rolled down tracks nationwide, fulfilling the purpose the derby's founder intended: to devise a constructive activity that fosters the parent-son relationship while teaching craftsmanship and good sportsmanship through competition.

—*From* ProSpeak, *December 2003, Vol. 17, No. 11*

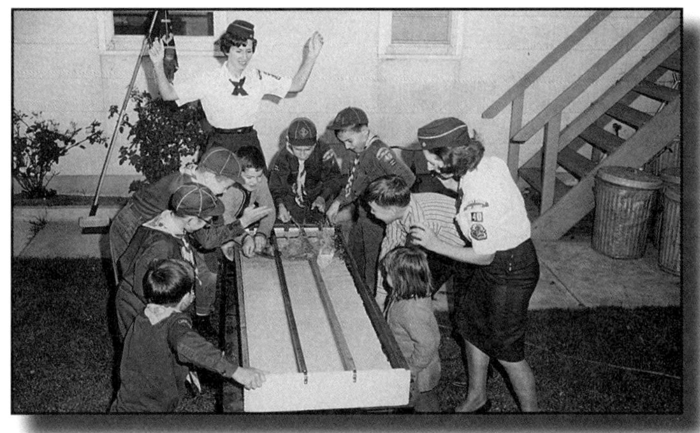

Cub Scouts raced model sailboats during this period, too, but it was not until 1958 that "Regatta Kits," the model sailboats often used in raingutter regattas, appeared in Supply Division catalogs. Kits for eight boats, including all parts, sails, and decals, cost $2.95.

For June 1955, Cub Scouting's suggested theme was "Wheels, Wings, and Things," and the summer *Cub Scout Program Quarterly* gave detailed instructions for building cars and the track and running a "Pack Meeting Derby." Kits were available that year in Supply Division catalogs; materials for eight pinewood derby cars cost $2.75. The *Quarterly*'s instructions for a derby advised pack leaders they also could cut and shape enough wood blocks themselves to make up a kit for each boy in the pack. The pinewood derby became the most popular monthly theme and an annual event in most packs.

Training for Leaders

During the early 1950s, all Cub Scout den and pack leaders received more program help. Cubmasters and den mothers got the *Cub Scout Program Quarterly,* compiled and edited by Marlin Sieg. Each issue included meeting outlines, ideas, and suggestions for each of three forthcoming themes, and also offered much useful advice for den and pack administration. Also featured were "Blue Ribbon Ideas" from den and pack leaders, photos of pack activities, and songs, ceremonies, and ideas used successfully by packs around the nation.

Training of leaders was upgraded, too. To introduce a new decade, a new Cub Scout leader training series was produced, using filmstrips with cartoons and illustrations. The training comprised eight sessions, each about two hours long, plus a 20-minute "See and Do" pre-opening for each session. The training outline was for a group session, but each session also had outlines for personal coaching and home study. Everyone completed sessions called

"Fundamentals and What Cub Scouting Is," "Program Planning," "The Den Meeting," and "The Cub Scout Achievement Program." Cubmasters and other men took a session on pack management and the pack meeting. Den mothers took additional sessions on the "Den Meeting Place" and "Den Mother–Den Chief Relationships."

Also in 1951 the first Philmont conference for Cub Scout leaders was held at Philmont Scout Ranch near Cimarron, New Mexico. The conference was for male leaders only, with a separate program provided for wives and children.

That did not please the women. Sieg recalled: "The women who were involved in Cub Scouting raised such a clamor about being excluded from these meetings that the second year's agenda included them in the program. Bud Bennett took the men and I the ladies for the separate sessions, and together we handled the mixed group events. Also, we had both men and women on our faculty."

Adult Leader Recognition

Den mothers, seldom recognized during Cub Scouting's early days, now were viewed as essential members of the pack leadership team. In 1956 the Den Mother's Training Award debuted. By this time, den mothers wore more fashionable attire than the roomy smocks of the 1930s. The new uniform offered to them in 1955 featuring a well-tailored gold or blue blouse and blue skirt.

Good Turns

The Boy Scouts of America did several Good Turns for the nation in the 1950s. Cub Scouts participated in all of them. Although statistics were not kept separately for Cub Scouts, Boy Scouts, and Explorers, Cub Scouts played prominent roles.

The first Good Turn came in late 1950 and early 1951 when two million pounds of clothing were collected for overseas relief at the request of the American Council of Voluntary Agencies for Foreign Service and the United Nations. The following year, 1.8 million boys placed 30 million "Liberty Bell" doorknob hangers and a million posters to remind citizens to vote in the 1952 Presidential election.

In 1954, millions of BSA members participated in a national conservation Good Turn. They distributed about 3.6 million copies of a conservation poster. Packs, troops, and posts undertook thousands of hands-on projects, planting some 6.2 million trees, setting out 55,000 bird nesting boxes, and preparing 41,000 conservation displays for public exhibit. In addition, BSA units completed thousands of other conservation jobs.

For the 1956 Presidential election, Cub Scouts, Boy Scouts, and Explorers again went door-to-door to distribute 36 million doorknob hangers and 1.35 million posters. The get-out-the-vote campaign was the largest Good Turn in Scouting's history to that date.

Two years later, the national Good Turn was on safety. BSA members delivered 40 million emergency handbooks prepared by the Office of Civil Defense Mobilization and placed 50,000 posters in post offices. The 1960 Good Turn was the third get-out-the-vote drive by the Boy Scouts of America.

Riding the wave of the baby boom and the enthusiasm of its leaders from the national Cub Scout Committee to the pack level, Cub Scouting enjoyed its fastest growth during the 1950s. The program began the decade with 766,635 Cub Scouts and 215,724 adults; by the end of 1959, the numbers had swelled to 1,822,062 boys and 634,101 adults. By the mid-1950s, Cub Scout enrollment had passed Boy Scouting registrations.

Chapter 5

THE 1960S: MAJOR CHANGES

By 1960, when the Boy Scouts of America celebrated its 50th anniversary, Cub Scouting was the largest organization for boys in the nation. But the dropout rate was high. During 1960, 2.7 million boys were registered, but the number at year-end was 1,865,120, a loss of 30 percent.

To find out why, the BSA's Research Service began a comprehensive survey of the program. The Survey Research Center of the Institute for Social Research at the University of Michigan was engaged to conduct a comprehensive study of the attitudes of boys and parents—those currently in Cub Scouting and former members as well. The national Cub Scout Committee, then chaired by Frank Brittain Kennedy, got the results in 1964.

The findings set in motion a major overhaul of Cub Scouting. Creating Webelos Scouting in 1967 was the most important revision. Webelos Scouting gave 10-year-olds a completely new program designed to offer a different set of experiences for these older boys and to prepare them for Boy Scouting. Also in 1967, grade level (third grade) was a new criterion for joining, along with age.

The New Webelos Scout Program

In 1967, after careful study of the Michigan research center's 210-page report, Cub Scouting's national leaders introduced a thorough revision of Cub Scouting to offer a greater variety in advancement opportunities. Different achievements and electives were created for boys working on the Wolf and Bear badges, the Lion rank was dropped, and Webelos Scouting was established for 10-year-olds.

For Webelos Scouts, the new program offered 15 activity badges that boys could earn by passing requirements in such diverse fields as engineering, geology, aquatics, and sports. However, in 1967 these activity badges were not required to earn the Webelos Award.

Webelos Scouts strove to earn the Webelos Award, Cub Scouting's highest award at that time, by passing tests designed to prepare them for entry into a Boy Scout troop upon their 11th birthday. The symbol of the Webelos Award was the Arrow of Light. The three requirements to earn the award were:

- Show that you are prepared in the Tenderfoot requirements.
- Visit a troop meeting.
- Get an Application to Become a Boy Scout.

A special Webelos cap and neckerchief set the Webelos Scouts apart from the Wolf and Bear Cub Scouts. The Webelos activity badges were silver pins, and the Webelos "colors" were introduced as a place to wear the pins. The colors consisted of a curved gold metal bar with "Webelos" printed in blue letters and three colored "tabs" attached. The colors were pinned on the right sleeve at shoulder level. The tab colors represented the whole Scouting program: gold for Cub Scouting; green, Boy Scouting; and red, Exploring.

The Webelos Scout insignia was described as "a light blue and gold fleur-de-lis embroidered on a dark blue background with gold border."

> Boys in Webelos dens, which were under male leadership, were encouraged to take at least one overnight camping trip with their fathers. As the program evolved over the years, these overnight campouts became increasingly popular. Most dens today spend at least two weekends a year in the woods with an adult leader and the parents or guardians of the Webelos Scouts.

The Purpose of Cub Scouting

As a part of the program revisions, the national Cub Scout Committee wrote a new statement of purpose for the program.

> ### The Purpose of Cub Scouting
>
> Cub Scouting is a program of the Boy Scouts of America for parents, leaders, and organizations to use with boys 8, 9, and 10 years of age for the purpose of:
>
> - Influencing the development of character and encouraging spiritual growth.
> - Developing habits and attitudes of good citizenship.
> - Encouraging good sportsmanship and pride in growing strong in mind and body.
> - Improving understanding within the family.
> - Strengthening the ability to get along with other boys and to respect other people.
> - Fostering a sense of personal achievement by developing new interests and skills.
> - Showing how to be helpful and do one's best.
> - Providing fun and exciting new things do to.
> - Preparing boys to become Scouts.

New editions of the basic boys' and leaders' books came out in 1967 as the overhaul concluded. The program revisions pleased pack and den leaders, who saw the new advancement opportunities, and particularly Webelos Scouting, as a means to hold the boys' interest through their years in Cub Scouting.

1967 Editions of Wolf, Bear, and Webelos books

1967 *Cubmaster's Packbook*

1967 *Webelos Den Leader's Book*

The Den Leader Coach

In 1967, men as well as women could be registered as den leaders. The new registration forms included spaces for both den mother and den leader.

A new position was created—the den leader coach. While a den leader coach was not required, an experienced den mother serving as a coach could do much to help the new den mother get a good start by giving her the confidence and help she needs—immediately—on her first day. The Cubmaster could delegate den mother or den leader contacts to the den leader coach.

The Development of Day Camping

The national professional staff had an infusion of new blood in 1968 when Edmond T. Hesser, a 25-year veteran of professional Scouting, joined Cub Scouting as an assistant director under Bennett. For the next 11 years, Hesser was primarily responsible for *Cub Scout Program Helps* and *Cub Scout Roundtable Helps* and worked with *Boys' Life* to produce the Cub Scout Program Notebook.

Hesser also had a host of other duties. One of them was to develop day camping for Cub Scouts. He remembered:

> In 1967, the BSA Research director, Kenneth A. Wells, had completed a national survey in which he found that 42 of our 510 local councils admitted that they held Cub Scout

day camps. Bud Bennett told me that we were going to visit some of these councils to find out what their Cub Scout day camps did and how they compared with others. We did that during the summer of 1968. I reported our findings and recommendations to the national Cub Scout Committee in October. They [our findings] were that the Cub Scout day camp programs were superior to other day camps in that they had Cub Scouting as a feature, which was a natural for day camp programs. The committee gave its approval and so did the National Executive Board, making Cub Scout day camps an approved outdoor program for Cub Scouting.

Bud Bennett then assigned me to develop a manual for Cub Scout day camping, which I did with the help of Ernie Schmidt, secretary of the American Camping Association, and Russ Turner, the BSA's director of camping. The manual later became the text for day camping schools and local councils as they developed their own Cub Scout day camps.

It was thrilling to see how day camps grew to the extent that by 1979, 410 councils conducted more than 1,800 day camps serving more than 300,000 boys.

As assistant director of the Cub Scout Division from January 1968 through August 1979, Ed Hesser annually prepared the *Cub Scout Program Helps, Cub Scout Roundtable Guide,* Cub Scout Program Notebook, and other Cub Scouting literature. He developed the Cub Scout day camp, physical fitness, learn-to-swim, and bicycle safety programs, and the Cub Scout leader training with national Cub Scout Committee members. Hesser conducted volunteer and professional training at the Philmont Training Center and Schiff Scout Reservation for 11 years.

An Eagle Scout, Hesser graduated from Eastern Kentucky University and also attended the University of Cincinnati and West Virginia University. He served councils in three regions for 25 years as Scout executive at Rochester, New York; Middletown, New York; Peckville, Pennsylvania; Fairmont, West Virginia; Geneva, New York; and Orange, New Jersey, before joining the national staff.

Having served nine years as camp director of the Rotary Handicapped Children's Camp at Geneva, New York, he became Cub Scouting adviser for the writing of all literature pertaining to Cub Scouts with disabilities.

After retirement, he continued to serve on the staff of pow wows, Cub Scout day camp schools, Cub Scout Trainer Wood Badge courses, and Cub Scouting seminars. He also served as an assistant Cubmaster of Pack 199 in McIntosh, Florida, where he lived after retirement. Hesser passed away on June 23, 1998.

The Cub Scout Space Derby Begins

Cub Scouting entered the space age during the 1960s, adding the space derby to its regular program opportunities. Like the pinewood derby, the space derby involved a cooperative effort by parents and sons. Using a kit from the BSA's Supply Division, parent and son worked together to create a miniature spaceship powered by a rubber band–driven propeller that flew along a guy wire.

The first space derby kits were offered in 1961. Soon thousands of packs were scheduling derbies for aspiring young astronauts. While the space derby has not supplanted the pinewood derby in popularity, many packs now have annual races for spaceships.

Cub Scout Leader Training Is Revised

In the early 1960s, Cub Scout Leader Basic Training was revised. Basic training, given to all leaders, consisted of three two-hour sessions designed to give leaders fundamental information as quickly as possible after they were recruited. After basic training, den mothers and pack leaders had to take three more two-hour sessions, which helped to develop their ability to work with younger boys, parents, and other Scouters.

Three training awards were available for leaders—the Scouter's Key for Cubmasters, the Den Mother's Training Award, and the Scouter's Training Award. Cubmasters and other Cub Scout pack leaders had to complete basic training plus their position training and attend a pow wow, serve three years in the position, and complete a variety of projects. Den mothers had similar requirements, but with two years' tenure.

The new *Pow Wow Guide* book served as a guide to leaders who conducted this annual training event. Pow wow consisted of four subjects in Cub Scouting: Cub Scout games; crafts for Cub Scouts; pack administration; and skits, puppets, and ceremonies. It was suggested that each of these four subjects be two hours long. Each subject also had its own pow wow book that served as a guide for the pow wow session leaders and also as a reference book for den mothers and pack leaders after the course.

In 1967, new training had to be developed to coincide with the introduction of the Webelos den and the Webelos den leader position, as well as the new position of the den leader coach. Completion of Cub Scout Leader Basic Training took 8½ hours for most positions, with the den leaders and their assistants and den leader coaches receiving an additional two hours of specialized training.

There were separate sections for den leaders and pack leaders. Hands-on training was greatly emphasized, with part of every session devoted to games, songs, skits, or puzzles.

The National Cub Scout Committee Changes Its Role

The 1960s brought significant changes to the makeup and role of the national Cub Scout Committee. John C. Horn, a committee member, remembered that Bud Bennett, Cub Scouting director, grew increasingly dissatisfied and restless as the decade wore on. Horn recalled:

> "Things were just not moving as he felt they might or maybe should. Off-hour conversations with Bud centered in this area of restlessness. On occasion, he would ask whether this or that should be changed in the Cub Scouting program.
>
> "Finally, Bud remarked, 'Do you suppose that our committee members are not close enough to the boy and the den?' That spark was all that was needed, and in 1968 he suggested that we bring to the committee some women who had firsthand knowledge of the den and working with boys. That plan was consummated in 1969 and proved to be what had been missing for some time. The change in the membership of the national committee was far more significant than anyone dreamed. It not only brought a most important group of people into the top committee, but did much to change the functioning of the committee within the structure of the BSA. The first two women appointed to the national Cub Scout Committee were LaVern W. Parmley of Salt Lake City, a leader in the Cub Scouting program of her church and director of the Primary of the Church of Jesus Christ of Latter-day Saints (Mormon), and Elizabeth C. Reneker of Chicago, who had a long record of service to the program and was the wife of BSA President Robert W. Reneker."

Horn recalled the national committee meeting of October 15, 1969, where Alden G. Barber, Chief Scout Executive, welcomed Mrs. Reneker and Mrs. Parmley to membership on the national Cub Scout Committee, reminding us that this was an historic moment, that these two women were the first women members of a national committee. With this change, Horn said, "The national Cub Scout Committee moved from being merely a review and advisory group into a working and functioning body, planning, evaluating, developing, testing, and approving for implementation."

Elizabeth Reneker remembered the women were accepted immediately as equals with their male colleagues. She said: "There seemed to be no difference in the input to the committee as far as male or female members were concerned. LaVern Parmley brought to us the concerns of her church, for which she was in charge of the General Board of Education. My responsibilities, beyond the regular committee concerns, centered around uniforms, and I became not only a representative from the Cub Scout Committee to the Insignia and Uniform Committee, but a full member of that committee.

"When I joined the national Cub Scout Committee, someone told me that I was joining one of the most important committees in the nation. That was true in 1969 and continues to be today."

During the 1960s, Cub Scouting added to its membership rolls more than a half-million boys and more than 100,000 leaders. At the end of 1969, enrollment stood at 2,380,336 Cub Scouts and 777,926 leaders and was still rising. But the growth rate was slowing as the post–World War II baby boom ebbed.

Chapter 6

THE 1970S:
BROADENING CUB SCOUTING'S REACH

During the late 1960s and early 1970s, the Boy Scouts of America made a concerted effort to extend Scouting, including Cub Scouting, to the poor, minority youth, and boys with disabilities. To reach the poor in the core areas of big cities and disadvantaged rural areas, the BSA began the Inner-City/Rural program in 1965. It was the largest research and development program ever undertaken by the BSA.

For six years, special projects operated, testing various methods of extending Scouting to the poor and minorities. Storefront Scout centers manned by professionals opened in several cities, and an aggressive campaign began to form packs and troops in public housing projects. Special efforts recruited among African Americans, Puerto Ricans, Mexican Americans, and Cuban refugees. At the same time, the Inner-City/Rural program focused on poor youth in Appalachia, the Ozarks, and other poverty pockets in rural areas.

The BSA strove with much success to shed its image as an organization primarily for middle-class whites. A large percentage of the urban poor were African Americans; during the 1960s and later, tens of thousands of African American boys were recruited into packs and troops. Inner-city and rural pack leaders got a new series of booklets called *Cub Scout Ideas,* each with two complete themes for four months of activities.

During the 1970s, the BSA put new emphasis on bringing Scouting to youth with disabilities. More than 60,000 young people with disabilities were enrolled in Cub Scout packs, Boy Scout troops, and Explorer posts operated by institutions and community organizations. An estimated 150,000 others were members of mainstream units. Booklets were produced to guide leaders in working with members who were deaf or blind or had other physical or mental disabilities. In 1974, the National Advisory Committee on Scouting for the Handicapped was established with representatives from leading national organizations and governmental agencies for people with disabilities.

In 1978, age restrictions were removed for people with severe disabilities so they could continue in Cub Scouting, Boy Scouting, and Exploring beyond the normal cutoff ages. (Age limits for people with mental disabilities had been removed in 1965.)

Heading these efforts was Robert L. Untch, who in 1971 succeeded Bud Bennett as director of Cub Scouting. A professional Scouter since 1943, Untch was a deputy regional Scout executive when he was appointed director of Cub Scouting.

Cub Scouting's fifth director, Robert L. Untch, was a native of Canton, Ohio. As a Boy Scout, he achieved Life Scout rank in Troop 25, operated by Canton's United Methodist Church.

Untch attended Mt. Union College and Kent State University. As a Scouting volunteer, he served as Scoutmaster, Air Explorer Squadron Advisor, and neighborhood commissioner.

He entered professional Scouting as a district executive in Canton in 1943. Later he served local councils in Toledo and Cleveland before joining the staff of the old Region 4 as a deputy regional executive in 1967.

Untch became director of Cub Scouting in 1971 and served until 1982. After leaving that post, he continued his service by becoming director of the Shaping Tomorrow project of the Boy Scouts of America.

During his 12 years as director of Cub Scouting, Untch guided many new initiatives and program developments. Perhaps the most dramatic was the beginning of Tiger Cubs BSA, a program for second-grade boys and adult members of their families, launched in 1982.

Working with Untch during his tenure as Cub Scouting's top professional were national Cub Scout Committee chairmen Donald Parry, Donald H. Flanders, Dr. Rodney H. Brady, Glendon E. Johnson, and Peter W. Hummel.

After his retirement, Untch continued his leadership in Scouting as a member of the board of the Longhorn Council in Fort Worth, Texas. He passed away in 2003.

The Cub Scout Promise Changes

In 1972, the Cub Scout Promise lost the phrase "to be square." Program leaders felt the word "square" had become dated. "To help other people" replaced the phrase. Since 1972 the Cub Scout Promise has been:

I, (name), promise to do my best
To do my duty to God and my country,
To help other people, and
To obey the Law of the Pack.

Many program initiatives marked the "Untch era" of Cub Scouting. Summarizing Untch's contributions, his assistant, Edmond T. Hesser, said: "He was able to instill in a host of top volunteers and professionals, in every region across the country, the desire to work together to provide the finest Cub Scouting program to attract and hold millions of Cub Scouts and their den and pack leaders."

During the Untch era, the national Cub Scout Committee, with its enthusiastic and capable leadership, ranked among the most active and productive committees of the BSA. New activities aimed at strengthening Cub Scout packs. The initiatives became major programs in carrying out the objectives of the Boy Scouts of America and meeting the needs of Cub Scouts and their families.

Advancement Program Revisions

Among the early developments of Untch's directorship was the advancement program revision launched in 1973. Changes in requirements for achievements and electives in Cub Scout advancement encouraged more outdoor activity by Cub Scouts and more family camping. Most of the changes related to the Webelos Scout program, with new requirements for the Arrow of Light Award, which had been known as the Webelos Award. These included specific requirements related to Boy Scout Tenderfoot requirements, as well as a requirement to earn three activity badges—Citizen, plus two of the following: Aquanaut, Athlete, Naturalist, and Outdoorsman.

Cub Scouts saw two new electives—Sports, and Water and Soil Conservation—added to the *Bear* book, while the Family Alert elective moved to the *Wolf* book. The *Wolf* book also modified three achievements: Achievement 5 became Tools (was Whittling); Achievement 9 became Home and Traffic Safety (instead of just Home); and Achievement 12 became Research and Books (instead of just Books). Elective 16, Water and Soil Conservation, moved to the *Bear* book in a swap for Family Alert. As a result, both Wolf and Bear had 12 achievements and 20 electives.

The age requirements for Cub Scouts changed in 1972. A boy could join and begin to work in the *Wolf* book when he completed the second grade or when he became 8 years old. Similarly, a boy could work on the Bear requirements when he completed the third grade or became 9 years old, and a 10-year-old or fourth-grade graduate could work in the *Webelos Scout Book.* He could become a Boy Scout when he completed fifth grade or turned 11 years and 6 months old.

The changes reflected in part some findings of a study of attitudes toward Scouting made by the research firm of Daniel Yankelovich, Inc. Researchers found that while a majority of Americans regarded Scouting highly, there were signs that boys, particularly those in the Boy Scout age range of 11 to 17, were losing interest. The findings, announced in 1969, resulted in sweeping revisions of the Boy Scout program. Cub Scouting was found to be more in line with the interests of 8- to 10-year-olds, and so its offerings required fewer changes.

The Immediate Recognition Kit introduced in 1973 provided a means to recognize a Cub Scout as he worked on achievements for Wolf or Bear rank. He received a plastic diamond-shaped emblem to wear buttoned onto the right shirt pocket. When he completed three achievements, he got a yellow (Wolf) or red (Bear) bead for attaching to the "Progress Toward Rank" emblem with a length of yellow plastic lace. This special recognition encouraged Cub Scouts to complete all parts of the achievements. When a boy had earned four beads, he had completed his rank requirements and would be recognized at the next pack meeting with his Wolf or Bear badge.

In 1978, five ranks were established for Cub Scouting: Bobcat, Wolf, Bear, Webelos, and Arrow of Light Award. The Webelos badge became the fourth rank and Webelos Scouts began to work on this award as soon as they completed the fourth grade or turned 10 years old. The requirements for earning these awards were revised, and included learning many of the things a Webelos Scout would need to know to prepare him to become a Boy Scout at the end of his fifth-grade year or when he became 11.

The cloth Webelos badge was introduced to be worn centered on the bottom of the left uniform pocket to complete a diamond of cloth badges. A Webelos Scout could begin work on the Arrow of Light Award as soon as he earned the Webelos badge. The Arrow of Light Award was a cloth badge worn on the left pocket flap of the Cub Scout uniform. It is the only Cub Scout badge worn on the Boy Scout uniform, just below the left pocket.

New Programs Introduced

Cub Scout Bicycle Safety Program

Several new programs began in the 1970s to add new interest at the pack and den level. In 1974, Ed Hesser helped to develop the Cub Scout Bicycle Safety program in cooperation with the National Safety Council, the Schwinn Bicycle Company, Sears Roebuck and Company, and the Bicycle Association of America. The program taught Cub Scouts traffic signs and the rules of the road, and how to maintain their bicycles, ride them safely, and have a lot of fun while doing it. Packs were urged to hold a bicycle safety clinic in their neighborhoods and a bike rodeo just for fun. Recognitions included decals for those who completed the safety inspection. Dens and packs also used plaster-casting molds available for each rank to make neckerchief slides for recognition. One monthly theme each year addressed bicycle safety.

Cub Scout Physical Fitness Championships

Also introduced in 1974 was the National Cub Scout Physical Fitness Championship. This event emphasized the importance of being physically fit. Cub Scouts would be tested on strength, coordination, and ability. Physical fitness events were suggested for packs, districts, and councils. This program, developed by Ed Hesser, helped meet a national need to improve boys' physical abilities in preparation for entering the President's Physical Fitness Program in elementary schools across the country at age 10.

Each Cub Scout and Webelos Scout participated in five events—standing broad jump, softball throw, push-ups, sit-ups, and a 50-yard dash. Boys earned points for completing each event. Recognitions included gold, silver, and bronze medals that boys could wear on their uniforms.

Push-ups

Sit-ups

A unique part of the physical fitness championships was that council-level championships followed pack competitions. Scores at the council level determined regional and national winners.

Rocket Derby

In 1973, Cub Scout packs got another derby—a rocket derby for miniature, but real, rockets. Packs could purchase rocket kits, which required a minimum of assembly, and a rocket launcher. Thousands of packs and day camps held rocket derbies for several years until the rockets were discontinued.

Scouting **magazine May–June 1975**

Cub Scout Learn-to-Swim Program

"Every Cub Scout a swimmer"—as part of the bicentennial program, Cub Scouts were encouraged to learn to swim so they could be "prepared for life." The learn-to-swim initiative was a natural for summertime program. The American Red Cross and the BSA cooperated in the effort to give swimming lessons to nonswimmers. Suggested teaching locations included not only lakes, but also community and school pools as well as motel and hotel pools.

Throughout the 1970s, Cub Scouts joined their older brothers in the Boy Scouts of America in an annual conservation project called Project SOAR (Save Our American Resources). Emphasis was on tree-planting, erosion control, wildlife habitat improvement, and other projects to improve natural resources. After the energy crises in the first half of the decade, attention turned to energy-saving projects. Particularly popular were collections of waste paper, aluminum, and glass for recycling to save the great amounts of energy required to refine raw materials.

Day Camp Schools Begin

Day camping for Cub Scouts by districts and councils grew at an explosive rate. The national Cub Scout Committee recognized a need for training key leaders in day camping. In 1975 the first national Cub Scout Day Camp School took place. This weekend course, held once or twice a year in each region, was developed to train day camp directors and program directors in the methods of day camping, including safety, administration, and program.

During the first three years of day camp schools, all participants took part in the entire program. Faculty members conducted the course using about 10 pages of outlines. In 1978 the national Cub Scout Committee created a task force to write a standard syllabus for the course. In the revised day camp school, day camp directors and program directors took separate sessions during part of the weekend to learn about their specific responsibilities.

Along with day camp school, day camp inspections began. Some Cub Scout leaders who had completed day camp school got additional training to inspect day camps. The inspection focused on safety, administration, and program. Those day camps that passed inspection earned a special ribbon.

Cub Scout Leader Training Revised

A new four-level training plan came out in the early 1970s. The four levels were orientation, basic, supplemental, and advanced (Cub Scout Trainer Wood Badge).

Cub Scout Leader Basic Training was revised in 1973. The new program had filmstrips and audiocassette tapes that were packed in a blue box along with a small filmstrip projector and cassette player. The box even had a little screen useful for smaller personal coaching sessions. The training used the coach counselor concept, borrowed from Boy Scouting. The blue-box kit was ideal for trainers, or coach counselors, to take to individual packs to train small groups.

Supplemental training included roundtables, pow wows, and five specialized workshops: a den leaders' craft workshop, den leader outdoor skills workshop, Webelos den leaders' activity badge workshop, den leaders' skits and puppets workshop, and den leaders' theme workshop.

In 1976 Cub Scout Leader Basic Training was revised again. The new training course had nine sessions. Cub Scout den leaders completed four two-hour sessions; Webelos den leaders, three two-hour sessions plus a weekend outdoor training course. Cubmasters and assistants had five two-hour sessions. Committee members and den leader coaches took four two-hour sessions. In addition, den leader coaches completed a four-hour Den Leader Coach Seminar. Training usually took place over several days, rather than have leaders complete training in one long day. Training could be offered as group training, personal coaching, or self-study.

Cub Scout Trainer Wood Badge

Advanced training for Cub Scout trainers was introduced. Wood Badge training had long been the province of Boy Scout leaders, and Wood Badge beads symbolized the best in Scouting leadership.

Robert S. S. Baden-Powell, the British founder of Scouting, held the first advanced training course for Boy Scout leaders at Gilwell Park Training Center near London in 1919. Wanting badges for the graduates, he thought of a huge necklace, some 12 feet in length, that he had acquired in 1888. The necklace consisted of more than a thousand South African yellow wood beads worn by the great Chief Dinizulu, a giant man of 6 feet 7 inches. B-P also remembered that during the siege of Mafeking, an elderly South African had given him a leather thong and told him that, if he wore it, it would bring him good luck. So Baden-Powell had his Wood Badge—a leather thong to be worn with two Dinizulu beads.

When Gilwell Park Training Center offered the first training for Cub Scout leaders two years later, in August 1921, graduates received a Wolf fang or claw instead of beads. This lasted only a few years. From then on, Wood Badge–trained Cub Scout leaders have had exactly the same insignia as Boy Scout leaders.

For many years, other countries sent their Boy Scout and Cub Scout leaders to Gilwell for training. Later, these countries established their own leader training facilities.

Wood Badge training, inaugurated in the United States in 1948 for Boy Scout leaders, became a strong force in motivating and training Scoutmasters, commissioners, and administrators. Wood Badge training was now accepted as an important unifying link in world Scouting.

In 1972, the national Cub Scout Committee responded to the need for Cub Scout Trainer Wood Badge and set in motion the necessary approvals to bring it about. The final effort for the training came in 1975 and field testing began in 1976.

William Elliott, a member of the Cub Scout Committee who spearheaded the development of this Wood Badge course, wrote: "When we first began to conceptualize the course, it was pretty clear that Cub Scout Wood Badge should not be an extension of basic training for pack leaders. We felt that pow wows, roundtables, and various other workshops held the curriculum for preparing den and pack leaders. We also decided that, even though they are great, the leadership skills in Boy Scout Wood Badge did not really have a direct bearing on (or in) the Cub Scout program, and we also felt that we would need to 'water down' the Scout syllabus by taking out the Scout skills, since they are not applicable in the Cub Scout program. So 'leadership development' didn't fit. Leadership development fits into the patrol method and troop operation, but not the pack and den. It would have been a mismatch.

"Then as we researched further, we discovered that the World Training Committee would really like for all Scout Associations around the world to have a 'National Trainers Course.' Bingo! It fit perfectly. So our Cub Scout Trainer Wood Badge is patterned directly after the *International Training Handbook*'s outline for just such a course. We have submitted our syllabus to the World Bureau and have received tentative approval."

The course got a walk-through in late 1975. Then in November 1976, the first course (900-1) was held at Camp Comer in Alabama under National Council auspices. Participants in this field-test course represented every region, and most of them became the core staff members of the first courses in each region in 1977. The national Cub Scout Committee gave final approval for the course in 1979.

Cub Scout Trainer Wood Badge had as its main purpose the training of representatives from councils in the methods of training and how to provide effective Cub Scout leadership development programs in their councils. Participants were required to subscribe to an agreement of service to this effect.

In addition to the service requirement, participants were asked to complete several study questions, including interviews with Cub Scouts. During the practical course, they wrote a "ticket," their commitment to apply their knowledge and skills to their jobs in their councils. After successful completion of these four parts of the course, participants were awarded the traditional Wood Badge recognition: two wooden beads, taupe neckerchief, and woggle.

Expanded Role of Women

The 1970s brought a greatly expanded role for women in Cub Scouting. In 1972, 38 den leaders were invited to the first Den Leader Coach Conference at the Schiff Scout Reservation. The following year, several previously all-male positions at the local council level opened to women. Women now were able to serve in virtually all Cub Scouting positions except Cubmaster and Webelos den leader and assistants. The restriction against women Cubmasters ended three years later.

Women also were receiving more recognition for their service. In 1971, a Silver Fawn Award was created for them. It was meant to be the women's equivalent of the Silver Beaver Award, which since 1931 had gone to male Scouters making outstanding contributions to Scouting at the local council level. The first Silver Fawns went to Elizabeth Augustus Knight, Marjorie Meriweather Post, and Ann Wilson Nally. Outstanding women Cub Scouters received a total of 2,455 Silver Fawns before the award was discontinued in 1974. After that, women Cub Scouters got the Silver Beaver Award along with their male counterparts.

In 1975, the first Silver Antelope Award to a woman, symbolizing exceptional service on a regional level, went to LaVern Watts Parmley from the Western Region. Other women who received this coveted award in the next few years included: Northeast Region—Solveig Wald Horn (1976) and Augusta L. Sanford (1980); East Central Region—Diane F. Mugrage (1980) and Mary Anne Rounds (1980); Southeast Region—Ann W. Nally (1975); South Central Region—Helen Hart Luckett (1978); and Western Region—Laurie O. Dievendorf (1980), Naomi Shumway (1980), and Martha Jo Behal (1981).

The first two women Cub Scouters to receive the BSA's highest award for adult leaders—the Silver Buffalo—were LaVern Watts Parmley in 1976 and Ann Wilson Nally in 1982.

Silver Fawn

Silver Beaver

Silver Antelope

Silver Buffalo

Uniforms Change

A new embroidered Bobcat badge came out in 1972. A metal Arrow of Light badge became an option to the cloth badge. Webelos den leaders got the option of wearing a new neckerchief, similar to the neckerchief Webelos Scouts wore but slightly larger and with a gold-embroidered edge.

Webelos den chiefs had the opportunity to wear a three-strand cord (blue, gold, and red) as recognition of their badge of office. Cub Scout den chiefs would continue to wear the two-strand blue and gold cord. Until the mid-1970s, the den chief cords were worn around the right shoulder, but switched in 1975 to the left shoulder so the Boy Scout's merit badge sash would not cover the den chief cord. At the same time, denner and assistant denner cords for Cub Scouts and Webelos Scouts also moved from the right shoulder to the left.

Two other uniform changes occurred during the 1970s. The uniform subcommittee of the national Cub Scout Committee, in conjunction with the national Uniform Committee, introduced a dress uniform for ladies in Cub Scouting. It consisted of a navy blazer with a detachable Cub Scout emblem, a light gray skirt, gold blouse, and blue tie. Men in Cub Scouting would wear a blue blazer with the Cub Scout emblem, gray trousers, white shirt, and blue-and-gold striped tie. The field uniform, however, was to be worn when working with boys.

The second change was the 1979 introduction of a square knot for those adult men who had earned the Webelos badge or Arrow of Light Award. The knot was red and green on a khaki background and bordered in yellow.

Wearing the United States flag emblem was optional for boys and adults. All Cub Scouts, if they chose to wear the flag emblem, were to wear it centered above the right pocket of the Cub Scout uniform. Adults in Cub Scouting would wear it on the right sleeve at the shoulder seam.

Cub Scouting reached its peak membership in the 1970s, then began a decline as the baby boom crested and waned. The crest came in 1972 when enrollment at year-end was 2,486,706 boys and 789,662 adult leaders. At this time, Cub Scouting had 51 percent of the total membership of the Boy Scouts of America. As Cub Scouting prepared for its gala 50th anniversary in 1980, membership stood at 1,711,237 boys and 547,471 adult leaders.

Chapter 7

1980:
CUB SCOUTING'S GOLDEN ANNIVERSARY

In 1980, Cub Scout packs around the nation celebrated Cub Scouting's Golden Anniversary. Wolves, Bears, and Webelos Scouts marked the program's 50th anniversary in gala fashion. Nearly every pack held an anniversary blue and gold banquet. Cub Scout actors recreated the contributions of Baden-Powell, Ernest Thompson Seton, Dan Beard, James E. West, and other Scouting pioneers. In thousands of packs, Cub Scouts played the games and practiced the crafts of the first Cub Scouts in the early 1930s.

Dens and packs also marked the Golden Anniversary with field trips, picnics, pinewood derbies, parades, and other special activities. Some packs appointed historians and compiled memorabilia from their own past. Others sought out and recognized the pack's alumni at open house meetings. Many councils observed the anniversary at Cub Scout day camps and recognition dinners.

At the national level, Webelos Scout Jason Roger Sherman of Bath, Ohio, represented Cub Scouting on the BSA's Report to the Nation team in February. Jason presented a 50th anniversary memento to President Jimmy Carter, a former Cubmaster. Many states and city governments adopted resolutions commending Cub Scouting for its part in American life.

In honor of the 50th anniversary, a two-hour prime-time television tribute to Cub Scouting titled "Scout's Honor" featured Gary Coleman, star of "Diff'rent Strokes." The U.S. Department of Agriculture (USDA) Forest Service commissioned artist Rudy Wendelin to produce a painting honoring the Boy Scouts of America on its annual Smokey Bear poster.

National Council Events

The anniversary also featured the largest blue and gold dinner in history. More than 3,000 people at the biennial meeting of the BSA's National Council in New Orleans enjoyed a blue and gold dinner with Richard Schneider, vice-chairman of the national Cub Scout Committee, acting as Cubmaster and master of ceremonies. Cub Scouts brought birthday cakes to each table and helped to light the candles.

During the 1980 biennial meeting of the National Council, new uniforms were introduced for Cub Scouts and leaders as well as for Boy Scouts and Scouters. The new uniform was the work of fashion designer Oscar de la Renta. For Cub Scouts, the chief change was the addition of baseball-style caps with different insignia for the Wolf, Bear, and Webelos years. Male Cub Scouters were offered khaki tan shirts and olive drab trousers or shorts, the same uniform as for Boy Scout leaders. However, Cub Scouters' shirts had epaulets with blue shoulder tabs while their Boy Scout counterparts had red tabs. Women Cub Scouters were given the choice of pale yellow blouses, worn with blue shoulder tabs on the epaulets, or all-blue dresses.

Another feature of the 1980 biennial meeting was the Family Forum, a series of 10 workshops designed to look with a long-range lens at how the BSA could contribute to one of the most vital resources, the family. A panel of experts in family life led seminars and fact-finding discussions on topics such as family rites and rituals, improving family communications, value clarification and transmission, and preserving family integrity. This Family Forum developed into an activity councils could use to present seminars and workshops to provide information on family relationships with an emphasis on how Scouting benefits families.

A highlight of the anniversary celebration was the registration of the 30 millionth Cub Scout since the program's birth. He was Tony Blakey, who joined Pack 7, operated by Camphor Memorial United Methodist Church in St. Paul, Minnesota.

Other Special Events and Awards

Boys, leaders, and families who were active in the program throughout the year earned special Golden Anniversary awards called the Cub Scout/Webelos Scout Award, Family Award, and Pack Award. Cub Scouts and Webelos Scouts who completed the requirements for the individual award received a 50th Anniversary neckerchief slide. Families qualifying for the Family Award got a certificate. Packs earning the Pack Award received a 50th Anniversary pack flag streamer. The Golden Anniversary logo appeared on patches and Cub Scouting's literature and became almost as familiar as the Bobcat badge. The national Cub Scout Committee's 50th Anniversary task force, chaired by Ann W. Nally with Jack Rogers as vice-chairman, planned national activities during the year.

The Golden Anniversary year was more than fun and fashion. During the spring, Cub Scouts joined Boy Scouts and Explorers in a national Good Turn for the nation's 1980 census, delivering fliers to houses and apartments nationwide urging citizens to participate in the census.

Cub Scouts as well as Boy Scouts and Explorers could earn the President's Energy Award during the year if they completed requirements on energy conservation. In doing so, boys learned how to save energy at home and took part in various den and pack energy projects. The award was a handsome certificate, with the U.S. Presidential seal, signed by President Carter.

Chapter 8

THE 1980S: PROGRAM EXPANSION AND THE INTRODUCTION OF TIGER CUBS

The decade of the 1980s began with the national Cub Scout Committee looking to the future. A long-range planning committee was appointed to study the results of surveys on a host of basic questions covering the program's effectiveness, the changing American family, the training of Cub Scouters, the content of Cub Scouting's program offerings, and other matters. The committee's work yielded nine basic premises for Cub Scouting's future development that the national Cub Scout Committee subsequently adopted as guidelines for its work.

The premises were that

1. Cub Scouting is a family program and changes in the family structure must be taken into account;
2. The white birthrate has dropped while the birthrates for blacks and Hispanics are growing, which means Cub Scouting must be prepared to serve more minority boys;
3. Because more activities compete for a boy's time, the quality of Cub Scouting's program and leadership must be outstanding;
4. Communications and relationships with the chartered organizations operating Cub Scout packs must be improved;
5. Recruiting techniques for adult leaders must show the rewards of being Cub Scout leaders;
6. Cub Scouting's programs must be kept flexible to meet the needs of boys;
7. The increasing interdependence of the world's people requires increased attention to the concept of Cub Scouting as a world brotherhood;
8. Because today's boys have greater educational opportunities at an early age, Cub Scouting's entry age should be reevaluated; and
9. Cub Scouting's programs should offer opportunities to develop a boy's expanding interests in the modern world.

With these premises in view, the national Cub Scout Committee was restructured, establishing task forces for each of the targets.

Here Come the Tiger Cubs

It is often said that history repeats itself. Early in the Scouting movement, James E. West and other early professionals wrestled with "the BSA's younger boy problem"; almost three-quarters of a century later, the issue of age at entry into the program again became a topic of discussion.

In the early 1980s, a time when it would have been considered inappropriate to label the discussion a "problem," the focus was more positive. The professionals charged with the success of Cub Scouting, and for its growth and rate of transfer into Boy Scouting, contracted the research division of Fleishman-Hillard, Inc. to create a survey. The Cub Scout Division was focusing on ways to improve both membership and retention through the Cub Scout years. Among other things, the "Foundations for Growth" study was to research if, and then how, Scouting could meet the abilities, needs, and desires of 7-year-old boys and their families. The results were printed in April 1981.

The survey concluded, not surprisingly, that boys wanted to have fun. It further concluded that parents wanted a program in which they could participate in activities with their sons, exposing them to a variety of experiences. Parents wanted simplicity, a flexible meeting schedule, and a chance to involve the entire family.

The development in the early 1980s of a program for 7-year-olds or second-grade boys—both the approach to the development and the program itself—proved to be a very different venture for the BSA. A group consisting of an elementary school principal, a district executive, three faculty members from the University of Minnesota, a medical doctor, a representative of Fleishman-Hillard, a BSA area director, and two members of the Cub Scout Division staff reviewed the Foundations for Growth survey results. They also reviewed other programs for boys of this age.

The group designed a program to match the desires identified in the survey with the developmental needs of boys this age. The primary concepts important to include in the program, the group believed, were boy-adult teams, shared leadership, a simple and immediate award (not reward) system, low cost, little structure, support of the family, and fun.

In May 1982, the Tiger Cubs, BSA program was introduced at the biennial meeting of the Boy Scouts of America in Atlanta, Georgia. Tiger Cubs would be boys who were in the second grade or who were 7 years old.

Boy-adult teams became basic to the new program's structure, for many reasons. Obviously, involving the adult with the boy during the Tiger Cub year paved the way to recruiting informed adults into Cub Scouting roles the following year. But the major reason for the pairing was to meet the developmental needs of a 7-year-old boy. The task force took care to seek current child-development philosophy and to design a sound program that addressed the physical, mental, and emotional health and development of a young boy. The direct involvement of a parent or other adult who was concerned with the boy's well-being was the program's cornerstone.

These boy-adult teams were to share leadership of the group. This would spread the burden of leadership and identify potential leaders for the future. It also would give the young boys a special time when it came their turn to be in the leadership spotlight with their adult partners. Each Tiger Cub would have this opportunity during the year. The primary reason for creating a program of shared leadership was to benefit the boys.

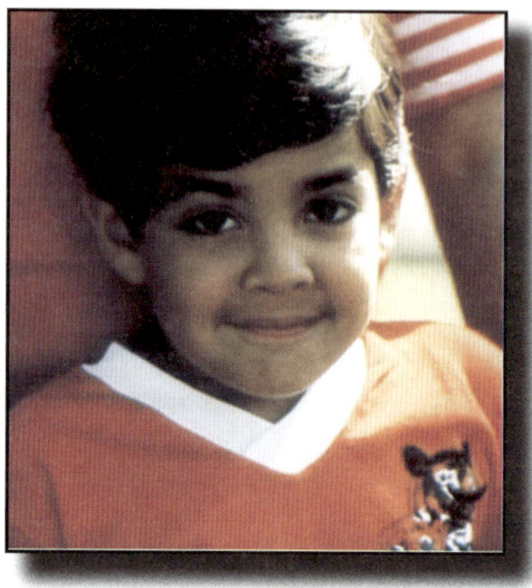

The Tiger Cub and his adult partner had a Tiger Cubs, BSA Family Activity Packet with a *Tiger Cub Family Activity Book* that had a program introduction and 17 "big ideas," plus a wall chart, iron-on emblems, and activity stickers. The uniform was simple. Tiger Cubs sported a cheerful tiger-orange T-shirt.

The group was to meet together once or twice a month, depending on the members' desires. Members were encouraged to make at least one of these gatherings an outing or a field trip. The *Family Activity Book* offered ideas for gatherings and group activities as well as family activities. The boy-adult team responsible for leadership that month was to plan and carry out the meeting(s).

The recognition system provided awards—not rewards—to recognize participation and reinforce pride in being active in the group. Focusing on cooperation rather than competition, each team had a wall chart to keep at home. The boy placed a sticker on the chart to record activities completed. The big ideas could be worked on at group meetings or at home with family members.

A unique component of the Tiger Cub program was that it affiliated stand-alone groups with Cub Scout packs. The group would be invited to visit one or two pack meetings during the year to see what the boys

The Tiger Cub emblem was the head of an adult tiger and tiger cub, symbolizing the program's stress on equal participation. The program motto was *Search, Discover, Share.* The Tiger Cub Promise was "I promise to love God, my family, and my country, and to learn about the world."

would be doing the following year when they joined the pack. Since this was a program of affiliation rather than membership in the pack, the Tiger Cub program was known officially as Tiger Cubs, BSA.

Tiger Cubs, BSA debuted at the BSA National Council meeting in Atlanta in 1982. Within three months, 77,000 Tiger Cubs were registered in the United States. The program's creators knew there was a need, and this was proof! Over the next few years, interest in Tiger Cubs, BSA grew, and councils across the country became increasingly convinced to support it. With no directive for individual councils or units to have a Tiger Cub program, it was up to local leaders to decide if they wanted to include 7-year-old boys.

The program was aligned with the school year in a program expansion in 1986–87, becoming a program for boys in the first grade or who are 7. The Family Activity Packet now included an activity book, an activity chart, iron-on logo emblems, stickers, and Tiger Tracks iron-on decals. An orange backing became available for a one-year service star to be worn on the blue uniform when a boy went into a Wolf den. A Tiger Cub graduation certificate and emblem also were available. Councils and districts had additional support materials, including a recruiting flier, *Tiger Cub Guidebook,* Fast Start training for Tiger Cub organizers, and several recognition items.

Expansion of Bear Cub Scout Achievements

Soon after the introduction of Tiger Cubs, BSA, the Bear Cub Scout program was enhanced. Twelve additional achievements were added in 1982 and published in a supplement to the *Bear Cub Scout Book,* making 24 achievement choices. Cub Scouts still had to complete only 12 to earn the Bear rank.

The new achievements covered such things as learning about one's religious faith, learning about law enforcement and local history, family fun, bicycling, conservation, cooking, model-building, sports, leadership, and learning how to handle money. The achievements were divided into four groups: God, Country, Family, and Self. The Cub Scout had to complete a specific number from each group to meet the requirements for the rank.

Baloo, the bear of Rudyard Kipling's *Jungle Book,* introduced the enriched program when the colorful new *Big Bear Cub Scout Book* was published in 1984, incorporating all 24 achievements and four new electives. The new book also gave boys the opportunity to use achievements not used for the Bear rank toward Arrow Points, providing greater variety and recognition opportunities for 9-year-old Cub Scouts.

Achievement 19, "Shavings and Chips," included a requirement to earn the new Whittling Chip card, which had a pocketknife pledge with basic rules for pocketknife use and safety. Those Cub Scouts who earned the Whittling Chip could also be entitled to carry a pocketknife during Cub Scout events, at the discretion of their leader.

Expanded Cub Scout Program

The expanded Cub Scout program was the result of several years of research and testing to find a way to serve boys younger than the current Tiger Cubs. A special study group, under the leadership of A. Roy Menzies of the University of Southern California, researched and developed answers to two major questions:

1. Should the BSA serve boys younger than the current Tiger Cubs, and if so, how?
2. Should grade, rather than age, be the prime determinant of when a boy joins and advances?

The study group considered several options, including a separate program for 6-year-olds. "The basic thinking was 'the last thing we need is another new program,'" remembered Ernest R. "Tommy" Thomas, associate director of the Cub Scout Division at the BSA national office. The study group finally recommended an age rollback to let boys enter the existing program earlier. The least complicated way to do this was to use grade, rather than age, for determining membership and advancement.

The first step, taken in 1986, aligned Tiger Cubs to first grade (or age 7) and the Wolf advancement program to second grade (or age 8). A slightly revised and simplified *Wolf Cub Scout Book* released in 1986 helped implement this change. On June 1, 1987, the second step took place, aligning the Bear advancement program to third grade (or age 9), followed by fourth grade (or age 10) for Webelos Scouts on June 1, 1988.

Flexibility in how chartered organizations use Cub Scouting has always been a part of the program. For example, using age alone as a requirement for membership and advancement best meets the needs in the Church of Jesus Christ of Latter-Day Saints. Age was retained as a backup membership requirement, therefore, to allow all boys to be served, including those in ungraded school situations and home-schooled boys.

Expansion of Webelos Scout Program

Expanding the Webelos Scout program to include both fourth-grade and fifth-grade boys was a major feature of the expanded Cub Scout program. The first group in this expanded program entered as fourth graders in 1988.

To enhance the Webelos program, five more activity badges were added to the existing group of 15. The new badges were Communicator, Family Member, Fitness, Handyman, and Readyman. The new *Webelos Scout Book,* published in 1987, also included some revised requirements for the original activity badges, and new requirements for the Webelos badge and the Arrow of Light Award. The new advancement program organized the activity badges into five groups. Webelos Scouts were required to earn activity badges from all five groups to earn the Arrow of Light Award.

For earning four activity badges beyond those needed for the Webelos badge, a boy received the new compass points emblem, an advancement incentive for Webelos Scouts to wear suspended from the right pocket of the uniform shirt. A small gold compass point pinned on the emblem signified each additional four activity badges earned.

The final step in the Webelos program expansion was a change in the Arrow of Light Award requirement so that a Webelos Scout could earn the award only after being active in the Webelos den for six months after completing the fourth grade (or becoming 10 years old) and earning the Webelos badge. This new requirement meant Webelos Scouts could not earn the Arrow of Light Award as fourth graders unless they were 10 and a half years old.

Fifth-grade Webelos Scouts were encouraged to interact more with Boy Scout troops through overnight camping, camporee visits, and other Boy Scout events. One concern of many Scoutmasters was that Webelos Scouts were not fully prepared to attend summer camp when they graduated from the fifth grade. To help facilitate this transition into Boy Scouting and summer camp, Webelos Scouts were encouraged to complete their Arrow of Light Award requirements before February of their fifth-grade year and join a troop at that time. This gave them time, as new Boy Scouts, to become acquainted with their fellow Scouts, to go on several weekend campouts, to begin to advance on the Boy Scout trail, and to be better prepared for participating in a troop summer-camp experience.

The new Webelos Woods outdoor activity aided in the Webelos-to-Scout transition. The one-day or weekend event, conducted by districts or councils, had Boy Scout leaders demonstrating to Webelos Scouts some of the skills they would need as Boy Scouts.

Expansion of Outdoor Program

The 1980s brought a renewed emphasis on outdoor activities for Cub Scouts. From the program's beginnings, leaders were urged to get their boys outdoors, in their own backyards and on day hikes. The earliest publications had instructions and plans for tents, shacks, and other shelters and for making ground beds, but leaders were cautioned against encroaching upon Boy Scouting by taking Cub Scouts camping away from home. This policy continued for 8- and 9-year-old Cub Scouts, but beginning in 1967 the Webelos Scouts were permitted to camp out with fathers and other adults for one or two weekends a year.

Webelos Scout overnight camping was now among the most popular events of a boy's final year in Cub Scouting. With the expansion of the Webelos program to two years, camping became even more important. Fourth-grade Webelos Scouts were encouraged to have one or more campouts. Fifth graders were to have more interaction with Boy Scout troops, including one or more campouts with a troop. This tie-in of Webelos dens with Scout troops helped to ensure that boys would continue in the Scouting experience by becoming Boy Scouts.

> The spectacular growth of summer camping for Cub Scouts of all ages enhanced the outdoor program. A Cub Scout day camp operated by a BSA local council was within easy reach of virtually every Cub Scout. (Day camps are one- to five-day programs for all Cub Scouts and Webelos Scouts, but do not include overnight activities.)

Beginning with publication of the *Big Bear Cub Scout Book* in 1984, family camping became an optional advancement requirement. Family camping was defined as camping by individual families, not groups of families, and was not under BSA direction or control. By 1988, however, some councils began to establish family camping areas at their long-term camps for Scouters, Cub Scouters, and families.

Resident camping for Cub Scouts and Webelos Scouts—a program for the boys and an adult family member—began in a few councils in the middle of the decade. By 1988, resident camping had been defined as a council-organized theme-related overnight camping program. It operated for two or more nights and was conducted under the leadership of a trained resident camp director and program director. Resident camping had to be conducted at a council-controlled camp and was open to Cub Scouts and Webelos Scouts from dens and packs.

A major change in 1988 expanded the role of women. For the first time, women could be Webelos den leaders and assistant Webelos den leaders. The policy on overnight camping by Cub Scouts and Webelos Scouts and their adult male parent or guardian also was changed so that the adult accompanying a boy could be male or female.

To ensure the best qualified leadership for all of these camping experiences, day camp schools expanded to include separate training courses for resident camp directors and program directors. All camps—day camps, family camps, and resident camps—had their own mandatory health and safety standards of operation.

New and Revised Literature

In 1980, the first of five Cub Scout Action Books was released, with the rest published within the next two years. They included the *Bobcat Action Book, Wolf Action Book, Bear Action Book, Action Book for New Scouts,* and the *Family Action Book.* This book series was designed to help youth in inner-city and rural areas advance in the Cub Scout program. These colorful books with their Spanish subheadings and multiethnic artwork helped to recruit and hold leaders and organize new packs, and touched the lives of thousands of boys.

The Boy Scouts of America has always stressed being prepared. In 1982 a new booklet called *Prepared for Today* introduced Cub Scouts to some of the things they might be faced with and taught some of the skills of how to be prepared to deal with them. Some of the subjects and one example of each included taking care of himself when he is at home alone (knowing emergency phone numbers), fixing something to eat (helping to prepare a meal), home safety (checking for fire hazards and family escape routes), taking care of young children (planning games to play with younger children), and problem solving (handling a bully). Cub Scouts who completed the projects received a T-shirt iron-on decal.

Perhaps the biggest change in literature was the *Cub Scout Leader Book* introduced in 1982. This book replaced five other books that were specific to a leader's position. The *Cub Scout Leader Book* helped to familiarize all pack leaders with each other's responsibilities and to build pack leader coordination and good working relationships. Published in loose-leaf format, it could be incorporated easily into a leader's Scouting notebook. The book included information on all phases of pack operation, job descriptions for every pack and den leader, a listing of literature, and a glossary of Scouting terms.

A second major new book, the *Cub Scout Leader How-To Book,* was published a few years later, in 1985. This book, under development for more than two years, combined new and updated ideas for den and pack leaders. Leaders now had one book instead of several in which to find games, crafts, skits, puppets, stories, and many special pack activities and events.

Webelos den leaders got a new book in 1987 when *Webelos Den Activities* was published. Each of the 20 activity badges had its own chapter with crafts, games, and other activities that helped to meet the requirements.

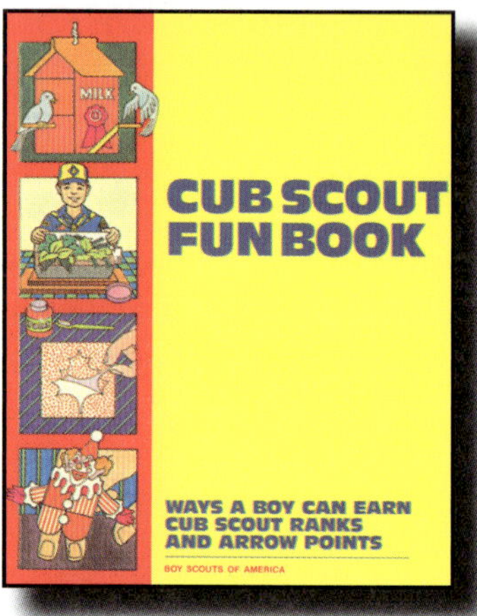

Besides these new books, the *Cub Scout Fun Book* was revised and updated in 1986. Many projects in the old book had become outdated or called for materials that were no longer available. This revised book, designed for use by Cub Scouts rather than leaders, also included links to achievements, electives, and activity badges.

New Programs

Cub Scout Sports

The first major addition to Cub Scouting's activity lineup in 10 years was the Cub Scout Sports and Physical Fitness program introduced in 1984. Burts Kennedy, associate director of the Cub Scout Division in the BSA's national office, said: "We feel this program is very appropriate because of the renewed emphasis on physical fitness in

> By the end of the decade the program would add more sports, including badminton, bicycling, fishing, gymnastics, skating, and ultimate.

this country. The experts are telling us all the time that youngsters in this age group need more physical activity, that they spend too much time watching TV, that many are overweight and out of condition."

Cub Scout Sports not only encouraged physical fitness but also enhanced the existing Cub Scout program. Sports offered Cub Scouts the opportunity to compete individually and in pack and den teams. In keeping with the Cub Scout motto, *Do Your Best,* participants were encouraged to learn teamwork and sportsmanship as well as the rules of the sport and how to participate.

The program began with 14 sports—archery, baseball, basketball, bowling, golf, marbles, physical fitness, skiing, soccer, softball, swimming, table tennis, tennis, and volleyball—with a manual available for each. A leader's guidebook to the program was available also. Individual Cub Scouts, as well as dens and packs, could decide which sport to pursue. Boys could take part in a sport, such as golf or bowling, on a strictly individual basis. They could play a team or individual sport and compete at a den or pack level. Boys also could take part in school- or community-based programs.

Recognition for participating was three-phased. A Cub Scout participating in a sport through his pack or community received a belt loop for his uniform. If he met the program's Physical Fitness pin requirements, he received the pin to wear on his Sports letter. And if he involved an adult teammate in the program, the adult also could earn a pin for civilian clothes wear. Once a Cub Scout had earned at least one belt loop and a Physical Fitness pin (later renamed the Sports pin), and involved at least one adult teammate, he qualified for a Sports letter, which was a large blue "S" with the Cub Scout and BSA emblems. This Sports letter was worn on a civilian sweatshirt or sweater.

Cub Scout Family Award

Established in 1980 as part of the Golden Anniversary awards, the Cub Scout Family Award continued to recognize families who participated in year-round activities, including attendance at pack meetings, serving on a pack committee, participating in a pack service project, and other pack and family activities. A special certificate recognized families who qualified.

CUB SCOUT
FAMILY AWARD

PRESENTED TO

OF PACK

CHARTERED ORGANIZATION DATE

Youth Protection training also became part of the revised Cub Scout Leader basic training that year. All leaders, whether experienced or new and just taking basic training, were encouraged to take this training.

Youth Protection

One of the "unacceptable" problems of concern to the BSA is child sexual abuse, an increasingly major social problem in the United States. In 1988 the Boy Scouts of America produced a Youth Protection training video as one means of bringing this problem and its solutions to the attention of all Scouters and to parents and the general public. The 90-minute film was divided in segments to allow for group discussions on the subject. The segments presented a series of realistic situations to help Scout leaders deal with the overall problem.

A booklet, How to Protect Your Children from Child Abuse and Drug Abuse: A Parent's Guide, was issued as a guideline for family discussions. This booklet would be included in all of the youth handbooks as they were reprinted. The ideas in this booklet would help youngsters learn how to avoid dangerous situations and what they could do if approached by a molester.

Other safeguards the BSA established included new guidelines on leadership, including the requirement that two adults must accompany all units on all trips and outings. The guidelines emphasized that no secret organizations exist in Scouting, and all forms of hazing are prohibited. At the same time, a new adult leader application form was devised, which gathered background information and references for new leaders. Chartered organizations used these references to help evaluate prospective leaders.

Uniform Changes Through the Decade

Beginning with the new uniforms unveiled in 1980 for boys and adults, several changes affected the uniform options and insignia placement.

In 1981, a light-blue neckerchief with dark-blue trim was introduced for Bear Cub Scouts. This neckerchief distinguished the older Bear Cub Scouts from the Wolf Cub Scouts. Now each program level had its own special neckerchief.

Many Cub Scouts and leaders had asked where they could wear the extra temporary patches they earned by attending day camp, Scouting shows, and other events. Boy Scouts had been able to wear a red vest for their extra patches. Beginning in 1986 Cub Scouts and leaders also were allowed to wear the red vest with their official uniform on all but formal occasions, such as blue and gold banquets and uniform inspections. Boys quickly adopted this vest to show off their myriad earned patches.

Cub Scouts were busy working on electives in their Wolf or Bear books. As they earned more Arrow Points, the question arose of how to display them all. The answer was that they could now wear their Silver Arrow Points in two rows under their appropriate badge and the Gold Arrow Point.

The BSA International Committee changed the requirements for wearing the World Crest badge in 1989. All youth and adult members of the BSA could wear this badge above the left pocket of their uniform shirt as a symbol of the world brotherhood of Scouting. A part of the cost of the badge was to be donated to the World Scout Foundation, which helps to develop Scouting in less privileged countries.

The expanded Webelos program prompted several changes to the uniform. Webelos Scouts would wear their activity badges on the light-blue front panel of their caps. The activity badges, redesigned, became full-color epoxy pins. The Webelos colors and the metal Webelos den numerals were eliminated.

A year later, in answer to overwhelming requests from volunteers across the country, the Webelos colors were brought back, this time with a straight bar on the top. The new Webelos colors were now worn immediately below the U.S. flag on the right sleeve.

Webelos dens got the option of selecting a name for their den instead of, or in addition to, a den number. If the den selected a name, the Webelos Scouts could wear the appropriate "den emblem" (a Boy Scout patrol emblem) in place of the den numeral on the right sleeve.

Webelos Scouts also were given the option of wearing the blue uniform they had worn as Cub Scouts, or wearing the khaki and tan uniform they would wear when they became Boy Scouts. They would still wear the Webelos insignia of the blue tabs on the epaulets, the Webelos blue belt, Webelos cap, neckerchief, and slide. The option of which uniform to wear was an individual decision by the Webelos Scout and his family rather than a den or pack decision.

At this same time, the U.S. flag insignia moved to the right sleeve of the uniform shirt at the shoulder seam. This was the same position as worn by all other members of the Boy Scouts of America. This meant, also, that Webelos Scouts who wore the khaki/tan and olive uniform did not have to move the flag insignia when they became Boy Scouts.

By the end of the decade Cub Scouters, too, had a new option with a blue and gold visored cap for men and women. Webelos den leaders and assistants wore the Webelos visored cap.

Training for Cub Scout Leaders

Trained leaders got new badges of office in 1980. When leaders completed basic training for their position, they could wear a new mylar badge with silver or gold metallic thread to signify their accomplishment.

Cub Scout Leader Basic Training was revised again in 1983. The training now provided four two-hour sessions for Cubmasters and assistants, Cub Scout den leaders, and pack committee members. Den leader coaches took four sessions plus the Den Leader Coach Seminar.

Webelos den leaders had two options for completing basic training. They could complete three two-hour sessions plus a Webelos Den Leader Outdoor Day, or they could complete all of the basic training in a Webelos Den Leader Outdoor Weekend.

That same year, the national Volunteer Training Committee approved a new Trained Leader emblem to be worn on the left sleeve of the shirt or blouse immediately below and touching the badge of office. Any leader completing basic training for his or her position could wear this Trained Leader emblem. The metallic or mylar badges of office used in the early 1980s were discontinued.

The four-level training plan introduced in the 1970s did not have a formal orientation for each leadership position. In the mid-1980s, a series of leaflets was published for use when recruiting leaders into new leadership positions. The new orientation materials aimed to get the new leader off to a "fast start" in his or her specific responsibility. The leaflets were "So You're a New Cubmaster," "So You're a New Den Leader," "So You're a New Pack Committee Member," and "So You're a New Webelos Den Leader." The pack leader was now required to complete Fast Start training for a pack to earn the national Quality Unit Award.

Training Option 1—a one-day course lasting six hours

Training Option 2—two two-hour training sessions with a workbook to complete

Training Option 3—self-study as a Cub Scouter's time allowed

A Fast Start video came out in 1987. The one videotape had separate sections for Cub Scout den leaders, Webelos den leaders, Cubmasters and assistants, Tiger Cub organizers, and pack committee members. When a new leader joined or when a leader changed positions within the pack, the den leader coach or another leader could give the new leader the video to view at leisure, preferably within two days of being recruited. The den leader coach or pack leader could then review the material and answer the new leader's questions about his or her responsibilities.

With the addition of more than 500,000 new members in Cub Scouting since the beginning of the expanded Cub Scout program in 1986—a gain of 25 percent nationwide—the need for trained, qualified leaders was greater than ever. However, at the same time, the number of single-parent and double wage-earner families made it harder to find people with the time and interest to serve as leaders.

A task force of more than a dozen volunteers from across the country, under the direction of E. O. "Robbie" Robinson, associate director of the Cub Scout Division, spent 18 months developing a new approach to leader training. A nationwide survey in 1986 made it evident that potential leaders did not have time for four or five two-hour training sessions spread over several weekends or weekdays. This survey and the efforts of the task force resulted in Cub Scout leaders having three different ways to take basic training.

In the first option, a group training course, all subjects were covered in approximately six hours. In the second option, leaders attended two two-hour sessions, then completed a home-study workbook. In the third option, a self-study course, leaders could take the required training on their own as their time permitted. All three options were based on the same newly formatted basic training. An integral part of the new training was a seven-part videotape with sections on Youth Protection, Cub Scout Sports, outdoor activities, rules and regulations, program planning, advancement, and finance.

Cubmaster Award, Den Leader Award, Webelos Den Leader Award, Den Leader Coach Award, and Cub Scouter Award

At the same time this new training course commenced, the Cub Scout Division instituted a new Cub Scout Leader Recognition Plan featuring a new set of awards based on training, tenure, and performance. These awards, the first designed specifically for Cub Scout leaders, consisted of a golden metal Cub Scout emblem suspended from a ribbon worn around the neck. The ribbon colors, like the colors of the individual square knots, varied with the specific award. The new awards were the Cubmaster Award, Den Leader Award, Webelos Den Leader Award, Den Leader Coach Award, and Cub Scouter Award.

Tiger Cub membership grew steadily after the program's 1982 introduction, from 84,000 in the first year to more than 330,000 by the end of the decade. With the addition of Tiger Cubs and the expanded Cub Scout program, membership grew by more than 25 percent during the 1980s. The decade began with 1,711,237 boys and 547,471 adult leaders. At the end of 1989, there were 330,625 Tiger Cubs plus 1,818,899 Cub Scouts and Webelos Scouts and 548,466 adult leaders.

Cub Scouts Do a Good Turn

An ongoing national Good Turn project began in November 1988 with the Scouting for Food campaign. In the first year Cub Scouts, Boy Scouts, Varsity Scouts, and Explorers collected more than 80 million cans and boxes of nonperishable foods for local food pantries and soup kitchens. The annual Scouting for Food drive is a two-week effort. Fliers—and in some cases collection bags—are left with households one week, and the next week the donated food is collected, counted, and delivered for distribution.

Chapter 9

THE 1990S: A DECADE GOING STRONG

As the 1980s ended, Cub Scouting continued to expand into new program areas. Cub Scouts enjoyed more outdoor program features. As more leaders joined the ranks, leadership training took a hard look at how to deliver training through the best possible methods.

The national theme was "Strong Values—Strong Leaders." Boys of all ages faced tough decisions about drugs, gangs, peer pressure, ethics, and more. The Boy Scouts of America, in providing a strong values-driven program, helped to strengthen character; develop good citizenship; enhance physical, mental, and emotional fitness; and develop good decision-making skills for life.

New Elements

During the 1990s Cub Scouting acquired many new elements, including Ethics in Action, Youth Protection training for Cub Scouts, a revised BSA Family program, a crime prevention program, and the addition of Cub Scout Academics to the existing Cub Scout Sports program.

Cub Scout Academics and Sports

The Cub Scout Sports program had met great success, but leaders and parents from around the country also wanted other, nonsports subjects. In 1991 the Cub Scout Division introduced Cub Scout Academics, in a format similar to the Cub Scout Sports program. Scholarship, like sportsmanship, leads to new adventures. It focuses on learning and skill development, not winning. Boys are encouraged to do their best.

The first four academic subjects were Art, Communications, Music, and Science. As in the Cub Scout Sports program, boys were encouraged to learn each subject on their own; with their parents, den, or pack; or in community-based programs. As they progressed through the individual subjects, they earned belt loops for learning about the topics. Then they could earn Academics pins for putting into practice the principles learned. If a parent or an adult partner earned an Academics pin along with the Cub Scout, the boy received the Academics letter, a large chenille "A."

Cub Scout Academics soon won approval from parents and leaders, and additional subjects were added. By the end of the decade the subject list included Chess, Citizenship, Computers, Geography, Heritages, Mathematics, Weather, and Wildlife Conservation.

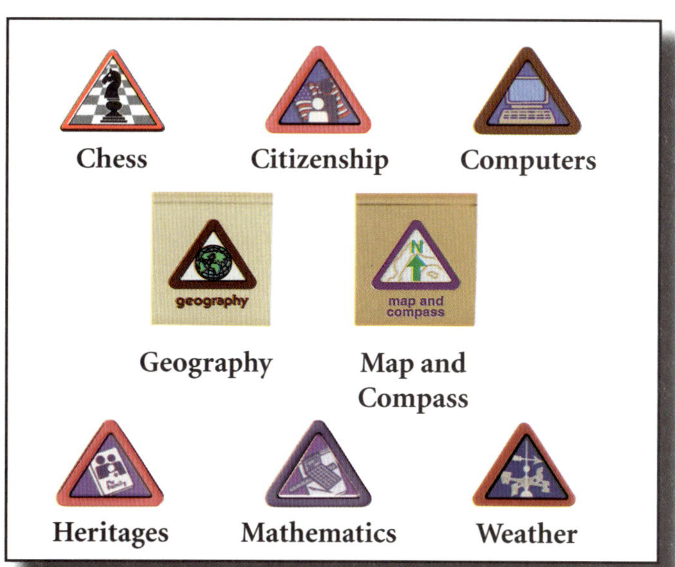

Cub Scout Academics pins and belt loops.

While new subjects widened the Cub Scout Academics program, the Cub Scout Sports program also expanded. Shooting Sports (including BB guns, air rifles, and archery) were introduced in 1993. A Cub Scout could earn Shooting Sports belt loops and pins, not in den, pack, or community programs, but only at council Cub Scout camps in a program led by a certified BB-gun range director. Shooting Sports did not have a separate booklet, as the other Cub Scout Sports had, but participants at camp received a separate instruction manual.

In a thorough overhaul of the Cub Scout Academics and Sports program completed in 1999, the requirements were simplified and made easier to understand, and all requirements were included in one book, the *Cub Scout Academics and Sports Program Guide.* Now, to earn a belt loop, the Cub Scout needed to complete the first three requirements for the specific sport or academic subject.

Late in the decade, the national Cub Scout Committee opened the Cub Scout Academics and Sports program to Tiger Cubs. A Tiger Cub had to have an adult partner accompany him, either working with him or as a coach.

Then to earn the pin, he would complete five of the next 10 or so requirements. A boy could also earn a pin more than once in a specific academic subject or sport, preferably by completing the requirements that were not met the first time.

As part of the changes, the Academics "A" and Sports "S" letters were replaced by a letter "C" (for Cub Scouts) where the Academics and Sports pins could be worn. The letter was simply a purchased item, with no requirements for earning it. Additional recognition items included a pocket card, activity medals, trophies, and a patch. Individual packs determined how these items would be awarded. Parents and other adults who worked with the boys could no longer earn an Academics or Sports pin or other recognition.

Ethics in Action

Ethics in Action was an activities program for Cub Scouts designed to reinforce the character-building goals that always have been a part of the program. Ethics in Action activities encouraged Cub Scouts and their leaders to "think a little deeper" about values and some of the decisions (and the consequences of those decisions) that are a normal part of growing up. The program was created in answer to parents' requests for help. The activities enhanced character formation—the development and reinforcement of the worthwhile qualities that are part of the Cub Scout Promise and Law of the Pack. The activities stressed cooperation and communication among the boys and between boys and adults.

The Ethics in Action program had 14 activity modules, each built around a single theme. The program also included two videos: *Ages and Stages,* which explained youth development; and *Reflecting,* an overview of the Ethics in Action process.

The principal process in Ethics in Action was the "reflecting" that took place after each activity. Reflection began with the leader asking specific questions that would lead the Cub Scouts to think about what had happened during the activity, why it happened the way it did, and what they might do the next time.

"We've always said we teach ethical behavior, and we do," explained Ernest R. "Tommy" Thomas, associate director of Cub Scouting. "But this gives us a system to work with, and that's something we haven't had before. People seem to be literally leaping to get started with it, and we're very excited about it."

Ethics in Action program promotion included special roundtable sessions and pow wow training sessions. After the original publication as a separate book, Ethics in Action later was incorporated into the *Cub Scout Leader How-To Book.*

Youth Protection

Child abuse is an increasingly serious problem in modern society, affecting every ethnic group, geographic area, and socioeconomic level. Keeping Cub Scouts safe and protecting them and their leaders are some of the reasons for the development of the Youth Protection training introduced in the late 1980s for all leaders in the Boy Scouts of America.

A video created in 1991, *It Happened to Me,* targeted the Cub Scout–age boy and his family. The video was intended to show boys—and their parents or guardians—what they can do to help prevent abuse from happening to them. Five scenarios showed different situations a boy might encounter. The video and program could be part of a regular pack meeting or den meeting. The *Cub Scout Leader Book* included a special handout for parents, to be distributed at the meeting. The handout served to help parents with parent-son discussions of the issues involved.

The Boy Scouts of America has recognized the importance of Youth Protection training. Since 1995, a requirement for packs earning the national Quality Unit Award is that at least one member of the pack must have completed this training.

Each copy of the boys' handbooks also included a booklet, *How to Protect Your Children from Child Abuse: A Parent's Guide.* The Bobcat requirements were changed in 1993 to include completing exercises found in the booklet.

BSA Family Program

The BSA Family program, which began during Cub Scouting's 50th anniversary celebration, got a more formal look with the 1990 introduction of the *BSA Family Book.* The program had two major goals: to strengthen families, and to encourage family involvement in Scouting. Weekly "family talks" were suggested. Families that completed the necessary requirements could earn the BSA Family Award during every 12-month period. Pins were available for all members of the family who earned the award, and Cub Scouts and Webelos Scouts who participated in the program could get patches.

BSA Family Awards

Guide to Safe Scouting

The *Guide to Safe Scouting,* introduced in 1991, provided health and safety guidelines for the Boy Scouts of America. This guide has been updated annually and is available on the national Web site so that leaders and parents may read or download the latest information on policies and safety guidelines related to activities.

National Den Award

The National Den Award was introduced in 1994 with the publication of a revised *Cub Scout Leader Book.* The award recognized dens that provide a quality year-round program. Requirements included using Cub Scout Academics and Sports, Ethics in Action, field trips and tours, camping, and service projects. Dens could earn the award once every 12-month period. The recognition was a ribbon streamer for the den flag or den doodle.

Crime Prevention Program

In May 1996, the Boy Scouts of America declared war on crime, joining efforts with organizations such as the National Crime Prevention Council, the National Sheriff's Association, and the International Association of Chiefs of Police. The BSA National Crime Prevention program helped young people and leaders with specific ways to stop crime. Young people would be taught safety techniques, crime reporting, and crime-reduction strategies. They also would learn avoidance strategies such as mediation.

The program capitalized on program already in existence. Cub Scouts—from Tiger Cubs through Webelos Scouts—had achievements, electives, and activity badges related to crime prevention. A Crime Prevention Award (a temporary patch for a boy's uniform, certificates, and a lapel pin) was available to every boy who completed the advancement requirements related to crime prevention, safety, and community awareness, and who also participated with his family, den, pack, or friends in a crime prevention project.

Outdoor Programs Gather Speed

Outdoor adventure—camping—hikes: these are the things a boy wants when he joins Cub Scouting. From the program's beginning, leaders were encouraged to venture into the out-of-doors, from backyard games to hikes. Many advancement requirements in the boys' handbooks related to outdoor program. Later, day camping and resident camping caught on. Webelos Scouts had parent-son overnight campouts. Families were encouraged to go camping on their own. Some councils set aside a portion of their camp, or specific weekends, when families could come to camp and take part in camp programs such as BB-gun and archery safety and marksmanship, crafts, and games. Some councils had "parent and pal" weekends at camp for all Cub Scouts.

By the end of the decade of the 1990s, it was apparent that Cub Scouts and their parents and packs wanted to take part in camping. In 1999 the national Cub Scout Committee approved pack camping. Under the leadership or guidance of a person trained in Cub

Scout basic outdoor skills, all Cub Scouts from Tiger Cubs through Webelos Scouts could take part in a pack overnight campout with their parent or other adult partner. These campouts had to be held on council-owned or -managed property, or could be held at city, county, state, or federal parks that had been preapproved by the local council.

Tiger Cubs Gather Steam

Tiger Cubs BSA underwent several changes and enhancements in the 1990s. Supporting the Tiger Cub group was a member of the affiliated pack called a Tiger Cub group coach. The group coach had a *Tiger Cub Guidebook* that explained all program details, and a flip chart to help introduce the program to a new group of adults when they joined. The Tiger Cub group coach also got a new badge of office.

As Tiger Cub groups grew, so did the need for training and recognition of the Tiger Cub group coach. Fast Start training for Tiger Cub group coaches was updated. In 1992, for the first time, Tiger Cub group coaches were included in basic training. A Tiger Cub Group Coach training award was introduced, along with an orange and black square knot. In 1993 the pack charter included Tiger Cub groups as part of the pack, rather than being "affiliated" with the pack. The adults were listed as partners—not registered leaders. This helped facilitate the transfer of "graduating" Tiger Cubs into the pack when the Tiger Cub year ended. The orange uniform T-shirt went from a V-neck design with white stripes to a round-necked, solid-orange shirt.

Program Enhancements

In 1995 the national Cub Scout Committee formed a task force to study the effectiveness of the Tiger Cub program and suggest enhancements. The task force found the program as implemented with the boys to be sound. The enhancements mostly took the form of record keeping, terminology, and support for adult leaders. Tiger Cubs were no longer "affiliated" with packs, but were members of the pack and listed on the pack charter as dens (although there remained a separate membership application for Tiger Cubs and their adult partners). Councils wanted this for ease of registration and keeping track of families. Dens were encouraged to meet twice a month (one den meeting and one Go-See-It outing) and to attend the monthly pack meetings. The Tiger Cub group coach was now called the Tiger Cub coach (since groups were now dens), with a blue uniform scarf and a new uniform emblem for the person holding this position. Boys also had an optional hat and a buckle for a blue web belt.

The iron-on paw prints were redesigned. Each "paw" had a cutout design representing the activity in which the Tiger Cub participated. The orange uniform T-shirt got a more modern look with a white neckband.

Except for an additional meeting night each month, most of these enhancements did not directly alter the program for the Tiger Cub. One thing that did affect the boy was the introduction of a belt totem—a paw-shaped piece of leather that attached to the blue web belt. The boy received white and orange beads for his totem when he participated in family and den activities.

While the inclusion in the pack, the increased number of meetings, and the instant recognition belt totem did not follow the thinking of those who originally designed the Tiger Cub program, considerable effort still went into keeping the program simple and relatively unstructured. Shared leadership, boy-adult partner teams, and age-appropriate activities without competition or pressure remained the program's cornerstones. Leaders still recognized that this was designed to be an introductory program for young boys and a caring adult to spend time together.

With springtime recruiting of Tiger Cubs now approved, age-appropriate day camp programming also was needed. These youngest members of Cub Scouting needed a summer program. Day camp schools incorporated ideas for including Tiger Cubs in at least a day or two of local day camps.

Tiger Mania!

Tiger Mania! publicity in 1995 thrust the Tiger Cub program into the spotlight. Considerable resources went into publicity and program promotion. Posters, banners, fliers, promotional pins, balloons, and resource packets for Cub Scout roundtable commissioners were distributed across the country. "T.C.," the new mascot, appeared everywhere. A local council could request the loan of a T.C. costume to use in its recruiting efforts. Packs had fun with these resources as they easily attracted new members.

Dens now had a *Tiger Cub Resource Book,* which included activities to accompany the 17 big ideas. *Scouting* magazine, *Boys' Life,* and *ProSpeak* all included articles about our orange-clad Cub Scouts.

Training Updates

In a continuing quest to meet the needs of new leaders, training required periodic updates. A task force of a dozen Cub Scout trainers from around the country formed in 1991 to review the current training material and make suggestions for a potential new course. Statistics showed that only about 21.3 percent of those leaders working directly with boys—den leaders and their assistants, and Webelos den leaders and their assistants—had completed training. It became clear that *how* training was delivered would have the greatest impact on the numbers of trained leaders.

A new Fast Start training was developed to give leaders immediate information to help them get started, understand what is expected of them, and establish effective meeting patterns so that Cub Scouts and their families could enjoy a quality program from the beginning of their experience. A new Fast Start video, produced in 1995, introduced "Max," the training dog who helped leaders understand their role and responsibilities. Web-based Fast Start training began in 1999, with access from national office–approved local council Web sites.

A new four-hour basic training course was introduced in 1994. The basic premise of the course content helped leaders answer three questions: What is Cub Scouting? What is my job in Cub Scouting? What resources are available to help me do my job? The course featured job-specific training for Tiger Cub group coaches, Cub Scout den leaders, Webelos den leaders, Cubmasters and assistants, and pack committee members. A new self-study manual also was written. The new training featured all-new posters and video. As new program features were added in the next few years, the basic training was updated in 1998 to include them.

A Continuum of Training

The continuum of training expanded with the Unit Leadership Enhancements included in the revised *Cub Scout Leader Book.* These were short training discussions conducted by the pack's own leaders as part of the monthly pack leaders' meeting. The leaders could select whichever of the 14 enhancements would best meet the pack's needs during the next month. Enhancements focused on advancement, recruiting, pack finances, family involvement, pack meetings, policies, Youth Protection, leadership training, and several other pertinent pack topics.

Another supplemental training opportunity introduced in 1994, called Quarterly Leadership Updates, offered a series of training sessions conducted by the district or council. Each quarter, leaders could get additional training on subjects touched upon in basic training. Three sessions were offered in each update, one focusing on Cub Scout principles, one on leadership fundamentals, and the last on meeting mechanics.

Previously, Webelos den leaders and den leader coaches had to take the same basic training that other pack leaders took, but also an additional training course. Determining when Webelos leaders and den leader coaches had completed basic training—and tracking who had taken what—caused problems for district training chairmen. To eliminate this confusion, all leaders now received recognition for completing the same basic training. The Webelos Leader Outdoor Training and the Den Leader Coach Seminar became supplemental training, which leaders still must complete to earn the appropriate leader recognition award.

> To help trainers plan additional training sessions that could be used at roundtable or pow wow, a publication called *Spotlight on New and Updated Cub Scout Program Elements* appeared annually. Each booklet had from five to 15 sessions, each of which was about an hour long, a perfect fit for a pow wow session.

With the addition of the Tiger Cub coach section of basic training, an additional training award was created, bringing the total of training awards available to six. One change in the requirements was that a leader must participate in a Cub Scout leader pow wow or attend at least four roundtables. By the end of the 1990s, the tenure requirements also were changed. Cubmasters needed two years' tenure (down from three), and all den leaders needed one year.

Cub Scout leaders got another supplemental training opportunity with three-day Philmont-style conferences held at the Florida National High Adventure Sea Base. While these conferences did not include family members, the course content and the total hours of training were similar to the Philmont conferences. Held in February, these conferences included popular Philmont training courses such as Cub Scout Roundtables, Cub Scout Outdoor Program, and Cub Scout Leader Training.

Training Den Leaders

A national Cub Scouting task force formed in 1996 investigated ways to improve the number of trained den leaders. The goal was to find ways to have at least half of all den leaders trained by the year 2000, up from the then-current figure of 20.1 percent.

To recognize the packs that made sure all of their Cub Scouts and Webelos Scouts had trained den leaders, the Training 2000 Award was launched in 1998 and continued through 2000. To earn the award, a pack had to have a trained den leader in every Cub Scout and Webelos Scout den. In addition, districts and councils, and their trainers, received special recognition if at least 50 percent of the den leaders in the district or council had completed basic training. The goal was raised to 60 percent trained den leaders for 1999, and 75 percent for 2000.

To help trainers deliver training, the task force created a special *Training Den Leaders* booklet containing "best methods" for implementing training. Training was recognized as the key element in helping den leaders deliver a quality program.

Literature Changes and Additions

Webelos Scout transition to Boy Scouting was an ongoing focus throughout the 1990s. Webelos Scout advancement was loosely tied to the joining requirements for Boy Scouts. A "Best Methods" plan for Webelos-to-Scout transition was published, based on a plan developed in the Denver Area Council. The basic responsibility for transition rested on pack leaders—the Webelos den leader and Cubmaster—and on unit commissioners.

An outgrowth of this focus on transition was a dual change in Cub Scouting literature. First, the plans for weekly Webelos den meetings, which had always been included in *Cub Scout and Webelos Scout Program Helps,* were moved into a separate publication, the *Webelos Leader Guide.* This book replaced the *Webelos Den Activities* book, which previously had carried additional ideas for Webelos activity badges. The new book included the activities in the older book as well as the weekly den meeting plans previously in the *Program Helps.* The book also included charts to help Webelos den leaders ensure that their Webelos Scouts were able to complete their advancement requirements toward the Arrow of Light Award.

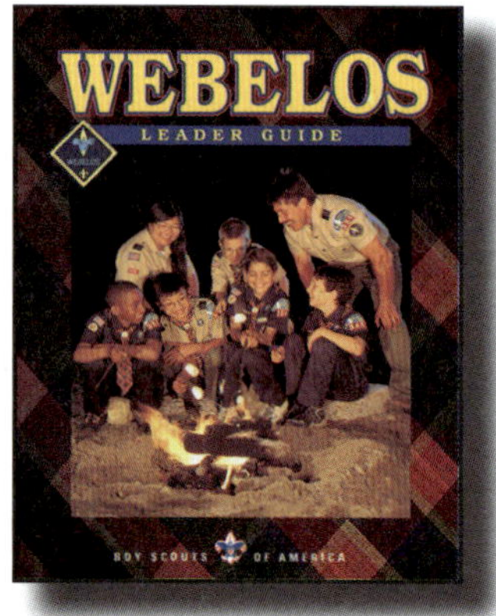

Another major change came with publication of the *1995–1996 Cub Scout and Webelos Scout Program Helps.* Before, leaders usually had to reference several other books to get specific instructions for the suggested activities. The new publication included all of the suggested games, crafts, songs, and other activities. Leaders needed only the *Cub Scout Leader Book* and the *Cub Scout Leader How-To Book* to complete their basic library.

A new ceremonies book, *Cub Scout Ceremonies for Dens and Packs,* came out in 1999. The book contained many new ceremonies and updates of older ceremonies that reflected the changes in advancement over the past couple of decades.

The Cub Scout Division and national Cub Scout Committee became the first in the national office to send out an electronic version of a publication so councils could modify a file. In 1993 the "'Take Any Council' School Night for Scouting Plan" was made available to councils on floppy disks and sent them to councils.

In 1995, *Boys' Life* magazine introduced a Cub Scout edition for Tiger Cubs and Cub Scouts through age 9. This new edition, geared to the reading levels of the younger boys, contained the same basic articles as the regular edition, but in an easier-to-read format. It also included a pullout centerfold poster with activities related to the current month's theme.

Membership Focus

Research by Louis Harris and Associates in 1997 indicated that even one year in the Cub Scout program provided a healthy, safe environment in which boys learned important values and developed self-confidence. The research also indicated the program provided a forum in which parents and sons could spend quality time together going places, doing projects, talking, and reading.

Garfield, the cartoon cat created by Jim Davis, became the official "spokescat" for a nationwide Cub Scout recruitment oath to God and country and leaving behind his quest for the ultimate lasagna. The two-year campaign reached boys who might otherwise not have had an interest in Cub Scouting. The campaign had news releases, yard signs, schoolroom presentations, and a special cassette of a Garfield "school principal" announcement for recruiting, colorful posters and fliers, and a variety of Garfield merchandise from the BSA Supply Division. The roundup slogan featured with Garfield was "Cub Scouting, because too much fun is never enough."

Cub Scout membership at the close of the 1990s reached a high of 2,181,013. This included 299,203 Tiger Cubs, down slightly from the beginning of the decade. Cub Scout membership was up to 1,016,421, and Webelos Scouts numbered 865,389. The number of Cub Scout leaders was up significantly to 572,719, reflecting in part the inclusion of Tiger Cub coaches as registered members of the pack.

Chapter 10

2000 AND BEYOND: CUB SCOUTING MOVES FORWARD

Uncertainty. Fear. Wars. Terrorism. Homeland security.

These words, to some degree, set the tone for the start of the new millennium. On the bright, sunny Tuesday morning of September 11, 2001, terrorists hijacked four jet airliners, crashing two into the World Trade Center in New York City, one into the Pentagon outside Washington, D.C., and the last into a field in western Pennsylvania after passengers attempted to wrest control from the hijackers.

Nearly 3,000 people died in a few short hours. Thousands more were injured.

In true Scout fashion, members of the Boy Scouts of America—Cub Scouts, Boy Scouts, and Venturers—acted to help those in need. In the Suffolk County Council, New York, Tiger Cubs helped packs and troops collect more than 153,000 bottled drinks for rescue workers.

According to a News Brief article in *Scouting* magazine, November–December 2001: "On Saturday, September 15, members of the National Capital Area Council responded to 'A Call to Action' by organizing flag-waving displays in a highly visible show of patriotism and support for the attack victims. In hundreds of locations across the metro Washington, D.C., area, fully uniformed Cub Scouts, Boy Scouts, Venturers, and leaders waved flags and displayed signs of sympathy, resolve, and support.

"In addition, Scouts accomplished many Good Turns by running errands and caring for pets of neighbors with a family member in the hospital, either as a victim or as a medical staff member."

Lukas (Luke) Grine, a Webelos Scout from Pack 187 in Baltimore, Maryland, went door-to-door and collected more than 400 pairs of gloves. He personalized them by stuffing a penny and a thank-you note into one glove of each pair. His pack took up his cause and collected another 800 pairs of gloves, all of which were personalized as Luke had done. The gloves were meant to keep the rescue workers' hands from bleeding, and the penny was for good luck.

Elsewhere across the nation, Scouts organized other flag ceremonies and patriotic events. Cub Scouts collected supplies for rescue workers. The Law of the Pack phrase about "giving goodwill" took on special meaning for Cub Scouts nationwide.

All across America, families took a closer look at disaster preparedness by assembling essential supplies such as water, food, first aid supplies, tools, clothing, evacuation route maps, and contact information. Through the Emergency Preparedness BSA program, Cub Scouts learned about protecting themselves in case of a disaster. The program stressed preparedness by individuals, the family, and the community. It was developed in conjunction with the United States Department of Homeland Security to prepare for emergencies of all kinds. An age-appropriate award was available for all levels of Scouting, from Tiger Cubs through adults. The requirements for all Cub Scouts included completing specific advancement requirements and taking an age-appropriate first aid course.

In Cub Scouting, changes happened rapidly. Character Connections® and core values were introduced. "Tiger Cub" became a rank. Training was completely revised. Cub Scout Leave No Trace Frontcountry Guidelines were introduced, with a patch for participation. Pack camping was approved, along with new training to ensure health and safety. The Boy Scouts of America started a new national Good Turn in 2004 called "Good Turn for America." The national Cub Scout Committee also planned for a major celebration from late 2004 through 2005 to mark the 75th Anniversary of Cub Scouting.

"Cub Scouting—Fun at Every Turn" was the theme for the early 2000s. The theme featured three characters: T.C. (a tiger), Akela (a wolf), and Baloo (a bear). The theme unified recruiting, the new "Power Pack Pals" comic books, and other literature and programs.

Character Connections and Core Values

Since its origin, the Scouting program has been an educational experience concerned with values. From the beginning, Cub Scouting was designed to build character, personal fitness, practical skills, and service.

> Character development should extend into every aspect of a boy's life and every aspect of Cub Scouting. Character development should not be viewed as something done occasionally as part of a separate program, but rather as a part of everything a Cub Scout does.

The goals of the Cub Scout leader related to character development were defined in two ways. The first was to seek out and maximize the many opportunities to incorporate character development. The second was to convince the young Cub Scout that character is important to himself and to his family, community, country, world, and God.

Character development involves at least three critical areas—knowing, committing, and practicing. In the Cub Scout program, using these three critical areas and relating them to values was referred to as Character Connections.

Character could be defined as the collection of core values possessed by an individual that leads to moral commitment and action. Cub Scouting's 12 core values could be used throughout all elements of the program—service projects, ceremonies, games, skits, songs, crafts, and all the other activities enjoyed at den and pack meetings. These 12 core values were *citizenship, compassion, cooperation, courage, faith, health and fitness, honesty, perseverance, positive attitude, resourcefulness, respect,* and *responsibility.*

Sue Weierman, a member of the character development task force of the national Cub Scout Committee, said, "We needed to connect the core values to the activities and advancements that the youth do so that, as den leaders or Cubmasters work with their boys, they have character development all through the program." Weierman added that she believed "any activity a Cub Scout is involved in with a parent or a den leader can be linked with a core value." Several of these core values relate directly to the Scout Law.

To make Character Connections an integral part of Cub Scouting, the boys' handbooks and advancement program integrated the 12 core values throughout. Several of the core values entered the advancement requirements in all of the handbooks, including the requirements for the Webelos badge and the Arrow of Light Award. The Bobcat requirements also were changed to include the core value of honesty. With each of the core values in the handbooks, a set of three areas—know, commit, and practice—provided specific discussion questions a parent or guardian and son could talk about.

At the same time Character Connections was introduced, the Purposes of Cub Scouting also were revised and simplified.

Positive Values

The 2004 revision of *Group Meeting Sparklers* included a statement of positive values. While fun is an important element of Scouting, leaders must remember that everything we do with our Scouts should be positive and meaningful. Activities should build self-esteem and be age-appropriate and should not offend participants or the audience.

The Purposes of Cub Scouting

1. Character Development
2. Spiritual Growth
3. Good Citizenship
4. Sportsmanship and Fitness
5. Family Understanding
6. Respectful Relationships
7. Personal Achievement
8. Friendly Service
9. Fun and Adventure
10. Preparation for Boy Scouts

Leaders in the Boy Scouts of America have a responsibility to model the organization's values and set a high standard for appropriateness in all Scouting activities. Leaders were advised to follow the high road when making decisions—if in doubt, take it out.

Activities are inappropriate and unacceptable if they include any of the following:

- Name-calling, put-downs, or hazing
- References to undergarments, nudity, or bodily functions
- Cross-gender impersonation
- Derogatory references to ethnic or cultural backgrounds, economic situations, or disabilities
- Alcohol, drugs, gangs, guns, suicide, and other sensitive social issues
- Wasteful, ill-mannered, or improper use of food or water
- "Inside jokes" that exclude the audience

Leaders were further advised that the lyrics to the following patriotic songs should not be changed: "America," "America the Beautiful," "God Bless America," and "The Star-Spangled Banner." Hymns and other spiritual songs should be similarly respected.

Tiger Cub Program Changes

Time marches on—and so does every program that once was new. Almost 20 years since its inception, the Tiger Cub program was now to undergo significant change. Again, the BSA looked to market research to decide the program's direction. As society experienced changes in lifestyle, family structure, and demographics, market research indicated a desire for the Tiger Cub program to evolve with it.

A task force of volunteers met in Nashville in the spring of 2000 to decide how to best meet the needs of a changing society and attract and retain the greatest number of families to the program, while remaining true to the intent of those who designed the original program two decades before. Task force members interviewed child-development specialists and sought to understand the characteristics and developmental needs of a first-grade boy. As the members designed an enhanced program, they took care to keep the developmental characteristics in mind. While program materials, resources, terminology, and recognition underwent significant changes, the actual activities in which the boys now took part were not much different from the activities in the 17 big ideas. Determined to keep the program simple to meet the boys' developmental needs, and also wishing to provide a program to satisfy those who participate in and implement it, the task force enthusiastically embraced the challenge.

The First *Tiger Cub Handbook*

Introduced at the BSA National Annual Meeting in Boston in 2001, the updated Tiger Cub program now had Tiger Cub dens that were fully integrated into the pack. There was now a Tiger Cub den leader, although the responsibilities were quite different from those of a Cub Scout den leader. Adult partners still participated alongside Tiger Cubs at every meeting and activity. One adult partner or another adult in the pack took the place of the Tiger Cub coach; this person was called the Tiger Cub den leader. The den leader attended all meetings and provided structure for the den's families as they shared in the leadership of den meetings and activities.

The Tiger Cub den leader was encouraged to wear a Cub Scout leader uniform, attend appropriate leader training, and attend pack leaders' meetings. Tiger Cubs still wore an orange uniform T-shirt but now had additional uniform options, including a newly designed blue cap with an orange inset, blue Cub Scout pants, socks, and a blue web belt.

The first *Tiger Cub Handbook* replaced the Tiger Cub Family Activity Packet. Instead of working on big ideas, the boys and their adult partners began to work through electives and achievements, culminating in earning the rank of Tiger Cub.

Tiger Cub Badge

The Tiger Track totem was redesigned to accommodate four colors of beads for boys who completed family and den activities, outings, and electives beyond those required for the rank of Tiger Cub. Since there was no appropriate place for the boy to display his diamond-shaped Tiger Cub badge on his shirt, the belt totem was designed to include a place for the badge to be affixed until he completed his Tiger Cub year and donned a blue Cub Scout shirt.

At any time after earning the Tiger Cub badge, but before earning his Wolf badge when in second grade, a boy must earn his Bobcat badge. This differed from any other rank in Cub Scouting; none of the others could be earned until the Bobcat badge was earned. The rank of Tiger Cub came before Bobcat because the requirements to earn Bobcat were not considered to be age-appropriate for boys just starting first grade.

Tiger Cub den leaders and adult partners got additional support materials. *Cub Scout Program Helps* began to include Tiger Cubs. The Tiger Cub den leader and the adult partner providing leadership for the coming month were encouraged to attend Cub Scout leader roundtable. The *Cub Scout Roundtable Planning Guide* now included resources for Tiger Cub den leaders, and the roundtable staff was encouraged to have resources for them in their monthly program.

> With the introduction of the Tiger Cub den leader and Tiger Cub leader-specific training came a new training award for the Tiger Cub den leader. The training award for the den leader coach was phased out by 2002.

Tiger Cub Uniform Changes

On August 1, 2004, the official Tiger Cub uniform underwent a major change. Tiger Cubs would now wear the regular Cub Scout blue uniform, including the shirt, web belt, and trousers. An orange neckerchief and Tiger Cub neckerchief slide were added. Tiger Cubs would still wear the blue cap with the orange front panel and the Tiger Cub logo. The orange T-shirt with the Tiger Cub logo became the activity shirt.

The Tiger Track belt totem was eliminated and a new Tiger Cub immediate recognition emblem was designed to be worn on the right pocket. The beads for achievements, electives, and required Go-See-Its would be worn on the new Tiger Track emblem.

With the new uniform, Tiger Cubs also wore the council shoulder insignia, unit numerals, the World Crest emblem, and the United States flag emblem.

Training in the 21st Century

To help more leaders complete training so they could deliver a better program to their Cub Scouts, the pack committee gained a new registered position: the pack trainer. This person was responsible for orientation of new families and pack leaders and for delivering Fast Start materials and information. The pack trainer could conduct basic training for leaders in the pack or encourage pack leaders to attend basic training presented by the council or district. The pack trainer also encouraged leaders to attend supplemental training conducted by the district or council, and to attend advanced training—Wood Badge. This person also kept track of pack training records.

Basic Training

Early in 2001, basic training completed a thorough revision. The concept of "seamless training" meant leaders could easily graduate through the training courses quickly and with little duplication.

The training began with Fast Start, completely rewritten and updated. The new Fast Start training (with separate sections for Tiger Cub den leaders, Cub Scout den leaders, Webelos den leaders, Cubmasters and assistants, and pack committee members) provided an immediate introduction to den and pack meetings, each leader's role in them, and the resources available to leaders. Fast Start also showed the role of the pack trainer, the new pack committee position introduced in 2000. Fast Start training was available as a video, or it could be taken on the Internet through the leader's council Web site.

The next step in the training continuum was a revised basic training taken in two parts. The first part, New Leader Essentials, offered an introduction in the values, aims, history, funding, and methods of Scouting to all leaders in the program—Cub Scouting, Boy Scouting, Varsity Scouting, and Venturing. This 90-minute session was ideally presented to volunteers in all programs at the same time. Leaders took this part of basic training only once. Having leaders from all programs take New Leader Essentials together offered convenient transition from one program to another. This also helped to remove perceived and artificial barriers among Scouting volunteers.

The second part of basic training was Leader Specific Training. In Cub Scouting, this training, like Fast Start, was geared for specific jobs in the den or pack. This part of training took 2½ to 3 hours. A leader was considered "trained" upon completing New Leader Essentials and the Leader Specific Training for that position.

Supplemental Training

Supplemental training continued to offer other specialized training courses, including pow wows, roundtables, and Youth Protection training. Webelos Den Leader Outdoor Training was updated and the title changed to Outdoor Leader Skills for Webelos Den Leaders. This course, following the pattern established with New Leader Essentials, was coordinated with the Boy Scout Introduction to Outdoor Leader Skills.

A completely new Wood Badge for the 21st Century was introduced for all leaders in Cub Scouting, Boy Scouting, and Venturing, and district- and council-level volunteers. The revised course focused on strengthening every volunteer's ability to work with and lead groups of youth and adults; it focused less on outdoor skills, which other courses already addressed.

Wood Badge

The five principles of Wood Badge for the 21st Century were

- Bringing the Vision to Life
- Models for Success
- Tools of the Trade
- Leading to Make a Difference
- Living the Values

Supplemental training also was enhanced. Some councils included Boy Scout and Venturing leaders with Cub Scouters in a daylong training event called a "University of Scouting." In most of these councils, the University of Scouting replaced the Cub Scout leader pow wow.

A new Trainer Development Conference was introduced in 2000. Like the older Train-the-Trainer Conference, the new course incorporated numerous contemporary training techniques and emphasized experiential learning, or "learning by doing." Participants got the opportunity to interact and practice what they had just learned. The course used a "BSA 500" racetrack-type game to emphasize and reinforce the experiential learning.

More Outdoor Program

In 1999, the national Cub Scout Committee had approved pack camping. Individual packs could camp at council-owned or -managed property, or in council-approved city, county, state, or federal parks.

To prepare pack leaders for pack camping, BALOO (Basic Adult Leader Outdoor Orientation) training began in 2000. To have a pack campout, someone from that pack had to complete BALOO training. In addition, each family group in the pack must have at least one adult at the campout. National standards were established for the approval of sites, similar to day camp and resident camp standards for health and safety.

Throughout Cub Scouting's 75-year history, age-appropriate activities have been stressed. The Tiger Cub, Wolf, Bear, and Webelos programs have progressively more challenging activities for the Cub Scouts. In the 1990s, the *Guide to Safe Scouting* spelled out additional safety guidelines. In 2002, the Boy Scouts of America created age-appropriate guidelines for most Scouting activities. The chart listed age- and rank-appropriate guidelines based on the physical, mental, emotional, and social maturity of youth members. The guidelines covered outdoor activities, sports, the use of tools, shooting sports, aquatics, and climbing, among other activities.

Wall climbing had become a sport in many schools by the new millennium. Boys who were in Cub Scouting participated in school and community climbing activities. Cub Scouts were allowed to take part in wall climbing and rappelling in controlled situations. All Cub Scouts could participate in bouldering and on commercial climbing walls, while Webelos Scouts were also allowed to climb vertical walls or towers.

In 2002, Cub Scouting introduced Leave No Trace Frontcountry Guidelines. Because Cub Scouts do not participate in backpacking activities, but do take hikes, attend day camp, and engage in other outdoor activities, the six guidelines were appropriate for these types of events. All Cub Scouts and leaders could earn Cub Scouting's Leave No Trace Awareness Award by learning about the importance of the Leave No Trace Frontcountry Guidelines, putting them into practice, completing outdoor-related advancement requirements, and participating in a service project.

The requirements for archery and BB-gun Shooting Sports were updated in 2003. Belt loops and Sports pins for these sports were available only through council-sponsored camping events with certified range officers. Tiger Cubs could complete these requirements while working with their parent or adult partner.

Leave No Trace® is a nationally recognized outdoor skills and ethics awareness program intended to reduce our effect on the environment. Leave No Trace is an awareness and an attitude, rather than a set of rules.

Literature Enhancements

The first few years of the 21st century saw several changes in literature. A complete revision and reorganization of the *Cub Scout Leader Book* made it easier to find information about specific programs.

The *Cub Scout Leader How-To Book* also was revised. The opening chapter focused on "accentuating the positive," the Cub Scout ideals, awards, and stressing good behavior. Another chapter called "Razzle Dazzle" included activities that spice up den and pack meetings—songs, sparklers, puzzles, stories, skits, tricks, and magic. The book had all the other favorites from the earlier edition—crafts, games, special pack activities, the outdoors, and working with boys with special needs.

All Cub Scout handbooks were revised. Some advancement requirements, including the revised Bobcat, Webelos badge, and Arrow of Light Award requirements, incorporated

Character Connections and core values. Other new or revised books included a new *Spotlight on Pow Wow* book to guide leaders of council and district pow wows and universities of Scouting. The *Webelos Leader Guide* was updated to include activities related to the revised Arrow of Light Award and Webelos badge requirements.

The *Cub Scout Songbook* and *Group Meeting Sparklers* underwent major revisions in 2003 and 2004. As mentioned, *Group Meeting Sparklers* introduced a "positive values" statement to help leaders build self-esteem in their Scouts as they have cheers and skits that are positive in outlook and do not offend any participants.

The BSA Family program, which dated to Cub Scouting's 50th anniversary, was revised again in 2000 with publication of a new *Cub Scouting's BSA Family Activity Book.* One of Scouting's aims is to develop its youth into participating citizens of good character who are physically, spiritually, and mentally fit. The BSA Family program is a resource to help families accomplish worthy goals while building and strengthening relationships among family members. Families could find ways to incorporate any of the hundreds of suggestions in the book into everyday family life.

As part of the continuing updating of Youth Protection training, "Power Pack Pals" comic books for Cub Scouts were introduced. These booklets were meant to give valuable instruction in an entertaining format for all young people ages 7 to 10. The first issue dealt with the subject of bullies and bullying. The second booklet covered Internet safety.

Soccer and Scouting Program

In August 2004, the National Council launched a recruiting program to specifically address recruitment in the challenging Hispanic youth population. The program was called "Soccer and Scouting" in English and "Fútbol y los Scouts" in Spanish. Councils that had used soccer when recruiting in Hispanic neighborhoods found it to be very effective. A soccer consultant was put under contract with the BSA to design a national program, write the materials, and conduct a pilot in a council with a large Hispanic market. The program blended soccer coaching and play with the Cub Scouting program, including advancement. A special Soccer and Scouting uniform was developed for youth in this program. Training was developed for coaches and assistant coacheson how to coach soccer play effectively as well as how to conduct the Cub Scouting program. An official pilot was conducted in Denver, Colorado, from June 2004 until mid-August.

"A boy who earns the Tiger Cub, Wolf, Bear, or Webelos Scout badge as a soccer-playing Cub Scout is as much a Cub Scout as any Cub Scout has ever been," emphasized Bill Steele, associate director of the Cub Scout Division, who worked with the developing program.

While this program was being designed specifically as an outreach to Hispanic youth, it was not limited to Hispanic youth. Highlights of the Soccer and Scouting program include the following:

- The year-round program is divided into four seasons. Each season begins with a recruiting/organization day ("interest generator day"), followed by 10 weeks of den and game-day activities, concluding with a tournament and graduation/recognition program.
- The den and the soccer team are the same thing; the pack is the league.
- Soccer and Scouting youth members wear soccer uniforms that also include BSA identification. Badges may be placed on the soccer jersey, which is part of the soccer uniform.
- A special Soccer and Scouting Program Helps booklet for each age group (rank), in both English and Spanish, provides information on coaching soccer and running the Cub Scouting portion of the meetings.
- Family-Time foldout posters with one side in Spanish and the other in English have self-help activities with requirements to be done at home for the various Cub Scout achievements.

Celebrating the Diamond Jubilee—75 Years of Fun, Family, and Friends!

Preparation for Cub Scouting's 75th Anniversary began several years before the actual event. Diane Cannon, a vice-chairman of the national Cub Scout Committee, became chairman of the task force to plan the anniversary events.

In the fall of 2004, every pack received a special 75th Anniversary envelope with copies of the requirements for the 75th Anniversary Award, the Outdoor Program Award, press release ideas, and a listing of 75 ways to celebrate this special birthday.

Many special 75th Anniversary souvenirs were planned, including a patch; pins; stickers, blue and gold banquet supplies such as balloons, napkins, placemats, and program covers; and other keepsake items. Plans included having a special activity booth at the 2005 National Scout Jamboree where there would be a series of activities and an outdoor play area.

During 2005, every Cub Scout, Cub Scout leader, family, and pack could earn a specially created 75th Anniversary Award. Requirements included participating in a pack, district, or council celebration event; learning about the history of Cub Scouting; and making crafts or playing games typical of 1930.

Cub Scout Outdoor Activity Award

A new award—the Cub Scout Outdoor Activity Award—was introduced in 2005 but is an ongoing permanent award. The first time a Cub Scout earned the award, he would receive a pocket flap to wear on the right pocket of the Cub Scout uniform. Each time the boy earned the award again, a pin would be added to the pocket flap. The award's purpose was to encourage outdoor activities in Cub Scouting, helping to increase attendance at day camp and resident camp, aid in the retention of Cub Scouts and leaders, encourage service and conservation of outdoor resources, and include core values in the outdoor environment.

Also planned were special events at the 2005 National Council Meeting in Grapevine, Texas. Suggested events included a pinewood derby, display of uniforms through the decades, and special collectors trivia question cards.

Epilogue

THE CHALLENGE FOR THE FUTURE

Uniforms vary, methods vary, but Cub Scouts around the world are much the same when they join the World Brotherhood of Cub Scouting and make the Cub Scout Promise. All are taught the ideals of Lord Baden-Powell: "When a fellow promises to do a thing, he means that it would be a terrible disgrace to him if he afterwards neglected or forgot to carry it out; in other words, when a Wolf Cub Scout promises to do a thing, you may be perfectly certain that he will do it."

For 75 years, tens of millions of boys have pledged to do their best. And for those 75 years, millions of adults—Cubmasters, den leaders, committee members, and family members—also have pledged to do their best to help those young people.

Today's Cub Scouts pledge allegiance to the United States flag with 50 stars, just as those Cub Scouts in 1930 pledged allegiance to their flag with 48 stars. Today's boys play games, enjoy sports, attend campouts, and take part in den and pack activities, just as Cub Scouts have done for the last three-quarters of a century.

Is the program the same as in 1930? Yes and no. The basic ideals remain—character development, citizenship, and personal fitness. Boys today still close meetings with the Living Circle. Cub Scouts promise to do their duty to God and country. They help other people—because they want to, because they have learned how to give goodwill.

Today boys have more opportunities, both in and out of Cub Scouting, than their brother Cub Scouts did in 1930. Cub Scouts use computers and have a world at their fingertips through the Internet. Like their earlier brothers, Cub Scouts like to cook outdoors and go camping. They play soccer and marbles. They bowl, ice-skate, and ski. They play musical instruments and create science fair projects. Today they learn about personal safety, drug awareness, crime prevention, and emergency preparedness. They take part in family discussions and help around the house and learn about their own personal past. Cub Scouts and their family members build pinewood derby cars, model sailboats, and space rockets. They have fun . . . with a purpose!

Cub Scouting has grown along with the boys who are members. Training has improved as technology has improved. Leaders can take advantage of training over the Internet. Today's leaders don't need a suitcase full of books to plan a great program, as our literature has consolidated and improved.

Today's Cub Scout program offers boys and their family members an opportunity to grow, to learn about their faith, and to take care of the bounty nature has given them. We know from many surveys that men who have been Scouts—Cub Scouts, Boy Scouts, Venturers—are better able to take care of themselves, their friends and family, and their communities.

We have challenges ahead. How do we recruit more boys and more leaders? What kinds of programs attract grade school–age boys, and how can the programs fit into the ideals of Cub Scouting? As we continue to improve our program, we must pledge to look at today's boys and try to understand their needs and desires.

Cub Scouting is 75 years old. Cub Scouting is fun at every turn. Cub Scouting—75 Years of Fun, Family, and Friends!

I, (name), promise to do my best
To do my duty to God and my country,
To help other people, and
To obey the Law of the Pack.

Part B: The Appendix

Appendix 1

MAJOR EVENTS IN CUB SCOUTING BY YEAR

1910 Boy Scouts of America incorporated on February 8. National Executive Board formed. Baden-Powell visited America to talk with leaders. President Taft became first honorary president of the BSA; Theodore Roosevelt first honorary vice-president.

1911 The National Executive Board recognized the need for a younger boy program.

1912 *Boys' Life* magazine became official publication.

1918 James E. West, Chief Scout Executive, secured the rights for the American printing of the British *Wolf Cub's Handbook* for sale to U.S. Wolf Cub packs.

1920 The First Biannual Conference of Executives emphasized the need for a younger boy program. First jamboree in England.

1924 The National Executive Board proposed "adoption of a younger boy program at the earliest date, should be kept entirely distinct from Scouting, should prepare for graduation into the Scout movement."

1925 William D. Murray named chairman of a committee to look into the younger boy program. Dr. John H. Finley and Dr. Jeremiah W. Jenks named to the committee. All were members of the BSA National Executive Board.

1926 First Silver Buffalo Award presentations made to Lord Baden-Powell and to the unknown Scout whose Good Turn brought Scouting to America.

1927 A portion of a Laura Spelman Rockefeller grant of $50,000 supported a research and development project on the younger boy program. Dr. Huber William Hurt named full-time executive for the committee, which was to "report to the National Executive Board at the earliest date."

1928 The fifth National Training Conference for Scout Executives held at Cornell University generated intense interest in the younger boy program. Experimental Cub units were started in each of the 12 regions of the National Council. In all, 106 locations nationwide were sanctioned for experimental Cub units.

1929 The National Executive Board approved demonstration Cub units. The Hurt committee prepared its definitive report and worked on the first Cub publications.

1930 The National Executive Board heard the Hurt committee report and approved the Cub program "controlled experiment" as of February 10. The board authorized Cub packs to register with the BSA starting April 1 for those packs qualifying under "special permit" requirements to assure adequate resources and leadership. Dr. Hurt and the committee were to monitor the program through its experimental stages. Inaugural Cub books included those for Wolf, Bear, and Lion ranks; *Parents' Cub Book;* and *Cub Leader's Outline.* Uniforms for boys were issued ($6.05 complete).

1931 First Silver Beaver Awards.

1932 First *Cubmaster's Packbook* and *Den Chief's Denbook.* Cubbing policies were published.

1933 "Experimental" restrictions removed as of May 25th; Cubbing to be "aggressively promoted as a part of the Boy Scout program." *Cub Leaders' Round Table* issued for pack leaders. Schiff Scout Reservation, Mendham, New Jersey, formally opened.

1934 A national outline for Cub leader training was offered, and the Schiff Scout Reservation hosted national Cubbing course three times. Bobcat requirements had changed and were much like those in use 70 years later.

1935 William C. Wessel became second director of the program, succeeding Dr. Hurt on January 2. All registered pack leaders received *Cub Leaders' Round Table* and *Scouting* publications. Local Cubbing advisory committees encouraged. "Leader-of-leader" training made available. Cubbing judged "excellent in every field of operation," including graduation to Scouting; reported to the Congress of the United States for the first time.

1936 Registration of den mothers made "optional"; before this year, den mothers not permitted to register. Smocks available for den mothers. C. Walter Seamans named assistant director of Cubbing. Cubbing reached 10 percent of the total of all boys registered in Scouting.

1937 Pack Financial Record Book developed; Pack Thrift Plan introduced. Full-year planning calendar issued. First *Den Mother's Denbook.* Cubmobile racer introduced.

1938 First International Cub Leaders' Conference at Gilwell Park, England. Bobcat pin introduced (for civilian wear). Den mother's badge approved. New den chief's shoulder cord. Cub Advancement Record introduced. *How Book of Cubbing* published. Waite Phillips made a gift of land in New Mexico, now known as Philmont Scout Ranch.

1939 *Cubbing Guidebook* and new manual for den mother training were produced. A Cub literature bulletin outlined all publications available to pack leaders. Donald C. Green appointed assistant director of Cubbing. Pow wows and roundtables began in many councils.

1940 John M. Bierer became second chairman of national Cubbing Committee, succeeding Dr. William D. Murray. Themes introduced into program. "Summer Program" pamphlet issued. Pow wows introduced as training medium. "Your Boy" promotion and Cub "goodwill" emphasis. Den chief training course launched. Gerald A. Speedy named assistant director.

1941 Webelos rank created for 11½-year-old boys with the Lion badge. Accumulated badges could be worn on uniforms, rather than only the most recent badge. Set of 10 pack organization charts issued for pack leader training.

1942 Cubbing responded to national war emergency. Boys allowed rank corresponding to age if late entry into the program (no need for catch-up.)

1943 In program literature, first reference by name to blue and gold banquet. Packs sold War Bonds and War Stamps. First Silver Antelope Awards.

1944 Literature and uniform shortages due to wartime priorities. Packs collected grease, newspapers, milkweed floss. Many packs with Victory Garden programs.

1945 "Cubbing" changed to "Cub Scouting." New bars for denners and assistant denners. World Friendship Fund established.

1946 A three-year study on appropriate ages for membership was launched that included conferences with leading educators and pack, troop, and post leaders.

1947 Uniform revision: long trousers for boys. *Scouting* magazine carried program outlines for leaders for the first time.

1948 All den mothers must register with the BSA (registration optional previously).

1949 William C. Wessel, director of Cub Scouting, died. Gerald A. Speedy named director; in November, Marlin Sieg named assistant director. Age levels for Cub Scouting changed to 8, 9, and 10, with boys entering Boy Scouting at 11. Achievement program restudied. At the end of the 20th year, for the first time Cub Scouting had more than a million boys registered at some time during the year, a 25 percent gain over the previous year.

1950 Cub Scout Promise changed to add the line "to do my duty to God and my country." A second international gathering of Cub Scout leaders held in Edinburgh, Scotland.

1951 Wolf book revised to reading level of 8-year-old boy. Other new literature: *Den Chief Training* and *10 Steps to Pack Organization.* A new Cub Scout leader training plan included eight training subjects using filmstrips, illustrations, and cartoons. First Philmont Cub Scout conference stressed basic ideas, policies, procedures.

1952 O. W. "Bud" Bennett named director of Cub Scouting. Philmont Cub Scouting course opened to women. BSA theme: "Forward on Liberty's Team."

1953 Den Chief Conference Plan approved and released. Cub Scout advisory group studied the Webelos Den Plan. First pinewood derby held in California.

1954 Robert N. Gibson named chairman of national Cub Scout Committee. Webelos den created for 10½-year-old boys. New Webelos den badge. Lion book changed to Lion–Webelos book. Pack numerals colors changed. Minimum age for den mothers and assistant Cubmasters changed from 18 to 21. *Den Chief's Training Conference* booklet printed.

1955 Pinewood derby becomes part of Cub Scout program. New den mother's uniform skirt and blouse offered. New Cub Scout pocket piece. New training posters. *Backyard USA* published for summertime activities, illustrated by Bud Bennett. Revised *Den Mother's Denbook* and *Den Chief's Denbook.* More than two million Cub Scouts registered during the year for the first time.

1956 Webelos day camp program introduced. Webelos advancement chart available. Den Mother's Training Award introduced. First Cub Scouting books in Braille. *Cub Scout Fun Book* and *Pack Committee* pamphlet published. BSA theme: "Onward for God and My Country."

1957 Increased emphasis on Cub Scouting for boys with disabilities. Bike safety highlighted. George C. Frickel appointed assistant director of Cub Scouting. Registered Cub Scouts subscribing to *Boys' Life:* 34 percent.

1958 New Cub Scout sports electives included skating and skiing. New *Webelos Den Book* with meeting outline helps for Webelos den leaders. Parent Review Party Kit prepared to bolster family participation in Cub Scouting. Bobcat pin approved for wearing on the uniform until first rank earned.

1959 H. H. Coffield named chairman of national Cub Scout Committee. *Cub Scout Water Fun Book* issued to help dads with dad/son activities.

1960 Golden Jubilee of Scouting and 30th anniversary of Cub Scouting in the United States. Special coin and patches issued. BSA theme: "For God and Country." Commemorative tribute in Washington, D.C., from fund contributed by Cub Scouts and Scouts across the nation. First den mothers' conference held at Schiff Scout Reservation.

1961 Den mothers' training program at Schiff. Comprehensive survey of the complete Cub Scout program initiated with Research Service spearheading this effort under the direction of Kenneth Wells.

1962 F. Brittain Kennedy named chairman of national Cub Scout Committee.

1963 Cub Scout Advisory Group considered many uniform variants, but recommended only the den mother's tie as an alternate to the neckerchief.

1964 National Summertime Pack Award created to encourage year-round Cub Scouting. Cub Scout Swim Plan introduced.

1965 For the first time Cub Scouting broke through the three-million mark for boys registered during the year.

1966 Cub Scout survey results influence deliberations of national Cub Scout Committee. Kenneth L. Miller named assistant director of Cub Scouting. Jubilee year for British Wolf Cub program.

1967 Cub Scout advancement program overhauled. Lion rank discontinued in favor of new Webelos Scout program with distinctive uniform and 15 activity badges. Den leader coach position created. School grade as well as age considered for joining requirement. William J. Jackson named chairman of national Cub Scout Committee.

1968 National Executive Board approved Cub Scout day camps. Membership fees increased to $2 for adults and $1 for boys. National staff included O. W. "Bud" Bennett, director; Marlin S. Sieg and Edmond T. Hesser, assistants.

1969 First women appointed to national Cub Scout Committee. Total registrations in Cub Scouting during the year hovered just short of five million people—boys and leaders. J. Bowling Wills named chairman of national Cub Scout Committee.

1970 Donald J. Parry, national Cub Scout Committee vice-chairman, acted as interim chairman. Bud Bennett retired as director of Cub Scouting. Project SOAR (Save Our American Resources) launched throughout Scouting. During the summer, 42 councils held Cub Scout day camps; National Summertime Pack Award stressed.

1971 Robert L. Untch named director of Cub Scouting. Donald H. Flanders named chairman of national Cub Scout Committee. Silver Fawn Award for lady Scouters introduced for presentation at council level.

1972 Cub Scout Promise dropped "to be square"; replaced it with "to help other people." First national Den Leader Coach Conference at Schiff Scout Reservation. New embroidered badges for Bobcat, Wolf, Bear, and Webelos ranks. Achievements and electives updated. *Cub Scout Day Camp* manual printed. Cub Scouts accounted for 51 percent of BSA youth membership.

1973 New Webelos den leader and Cubmaster neckerchiefs. Immediate Recognition Kit introduced. Cub Scout Leadership Development kit introduced. C. Joseph Nelson named associate director of Cub Scouting.

1974 Cub Scout Bicycle Safety and Cub Scout Physical Fitness programs introduced and emphasized. First regional Cub Scout chairman training at Philmont. Silver Fawn Award discontinued in favor of Silver Beaver Award for men and women.

1975 Cub Scout Day Camp School introduced. Webelos-to-Scout transition program launched. Learn-to-Swim program promoted. New literature for leaders of Cub Scouts with disabilities. Den chief's cord repositioned on the uniform.

1976 First national Cub Scout Trainer Wood Badge course in United States conducted. The God and Family and Metta emblems introduced for religious recognition in Cub Scouting. Dress uniforms redesigned for adults. National Executive Board approved women as Cubmasters and assistant Cubmasters. *Cub Scout Family Book* prepared and Cub Scout Family Award designed. Russell A. Williams named associate director of Cub Scouting.

1977 Dr. Rodney H. Brady named chairman of national Cub Scout Committee. Cub Scout program year changed to coincide with the school year. Cub Scout day camp inspections made mandatory. First regional Cub Scout Trainer Wood Badge courses held (six during the year). Audrey F. Clough named associate director of Cub Scouting.

1978 Five ranks established in Cub Scouting: Bobcat, Wolf, Bear, Webelos, Arrow of Light Award. Training awards updated. Family camping encouraged. W. Boyd Giles named associate director of Cub Scouting. Long Range Planning Committee for Cub Scouting appointed; 50th anniversary of Cub Scouting set for 1980 and a jubilee committee appointed.

1979 Wolf book rewritten. New Bear neckerchief. Family Vacation Training Project. Cub Scout Trainer Wood Badge course approved as standard training. Arrow of Light Award square knot introduced. Burts J. Kennedy named associate director of Cub Scouting. National Council moved offices to Texas. National Cub Scout Committee prepared for jubilee year in 1980; 50th anniversary literature included *Council and District Plan, Public Relations Plan,* and *Guidebook for Packs.*

1980 Golden Jubilee of Cub Scouting in the United States. The 30 millionth Cub Scout since 1930 was registered. First national blue and gold banquet at the National Council meeting in New Orleans. All packs participated in 50th Anniversary celebration. New designer uniforms for boys and leaders. Cub Scout Family Award now standard. New *Den Chief Handbook* and the first Cub Scout Action Books for boys in low-income, rural, and Hispanic areas. Family Forum introduced. A total of 410 councils held 1,800 Cub Scout day camps for more than 300,000 boys.

1981 Cub Scouts visited a national Scout jamboree for the first time at Fort A. P. Hill, Virginia. International tour of Cub Scout leaders to England. Glendon E. Johnson named chairman of national Cub Scout Committee.

1982 The 75th Anniversary of World Scouting. Tiger Cubs, BSA introduced at National Council meeting in Atlanta. E. O. "Robbie" Robinson named associate director of Cub Scouting. Robert L. Untch, director of Cub Scouting, promoted to director of the Program Group. Peter Hummel named chairman of national Cub Scout Committee. *Cub Scout Leader Book* published, replacing five other books.

1983 Jack Billington named director of Cub Scouting; Ernest R. "Tommy" Thomas, Jr., named associate director.

1984 Extended camping approved for Webelos Scouts. Cub Scout Sports program introduced. *Big Bear Cub Scout Book* introduced.

1985 The 75th Anniversary of the Boy Scouts of America; 55th anniversary of Cub Scouting. International tour of Cub Scout leaders to England. *Cub Scout Leader How-To Book* published.

1986 Cub Scouting expanded to serve all elementary school grades. Whittling Chip card introduced. Tiger Tracks introduced. Russell A. Williams Jr. again joins national staff as associate director of Cub Scouting.

1987 BSA Family program developed. Fast Start training video for Tiger Cub organizers. Cub Scout Sports now numbered 20. Jack Scott named associate director of Cub Scout Division.

1988 Webelos Woods introduced to aid in Webelos-to-Scout transition. February (or March) graduation of Webelos Scouts into troops encouraged. Five additional Webelos activity badges introduced, with a two-year Webelos program and a new *Webelos Scout Book.* Webelos colors discontinued. Ed Woodlock joins Cub Scout Division as associate director.

1989 Webelos colors brought back. World Crest emblem approved for wear by all Scouts and Scouters.

1990 Badge created for Tiger Cub coach.

1991 Cub Scout Academics introduced. Ethics in Action program launched. *It Happened to Me* Youth Protection video introduced. *Guide to Safe Scouting* created. BSA theme: "Scouting—A Bridge to the Future."

1992 Tiger Cub coaches included in basic training. Tiger Cub Group Coach Award added to training awards. Sam Skinner named chairman of national Cub Scout Committee. Gene Stone named director of Cub Scouting. Mark Griffin joined Cub Scout Division as associate director.

1993 New Youth Protection exercises added to Bobcat requirements. Pack charters extended to include Tiger Cubs. National Registration Service provides automatic "rollover" of Cub Scouts on June 1: first-grade graduates automatically listed as second-graders, second-grade graduates listed as third-graders, etc. Continuum-of-training concept launched.

1994 New four-hour basic training introduced. Quarterly Leadership Updates and Unit Leadership Enhancements added to supplemental training. National Den Award introduced. BSA theme: "Character Counts—Be Prepared for the 21st Century."

1995 Tiger Mania. Tiger Cub groups became dens. Fast Start training revised. *Boys' Life* created Cub Scout edition. Gloria Atkins named associate director of Cub Scouting.

1996 Tiger Cub emblem created to wear on Cub Scout uniform. Belt totem for Tiger Cubs introduced.

1997 Cub Scout Academics and Sports program opened to Tiger Cubs. Major revision of *Cub Scout Leader Book.* Female leaders allowed to wear either blue and gold uniform or khaki and tan uniform. G. Richard Williamson named director of Cub Scouting. Paul Lorenzini named chairman of national Cub Scout Committee.

1998 Cub Scout family camping redefined. Cub Scout conferences held at Florida Sea Base. Training 2000 Award introduced. Revised Wolf and Bear books introduced. Jerry Dehoney named associate director of Cub Scout Division.

1999 *Cub Scout Ceremonies for Dens and Packs* published. The letter "C" replaced the "A" and "S" for Cub Scout Academics and Sports; program underwent major revision. Pack camping approved. Last Cub Scout Trainer Wood Badge courses held. Brad Farmer named director of Cub Scout Division; Dave Proehl named associate director.

2000 BALOO training introduced. Pack trainer position introduced and den leader coach position eliminated. *BSA Family Activity Book* and requirements to earn BSA Family Award revised. "Climb on Safely" introduced to allow Cub Scouts to climb and rappel in a controlled environment.

2001 Character Connections and core values introduced; Ethics in Action program ended. Purposes of Cub Scouting revised. Training continuum revised to include New Leader Essentials for all leaders, Cub Scout Leader Specific Training, and Wood Badge for the 21st Century for all leaders in Scouting. *Tiger Cub Handbook,* Tiger Cub rank, and achievements and electives for Tiger Cubs introduced. Optional oval Webelos badge created. Tiger Cub den leader replaced Tiger Cub coach position; Tiger Cub Den Leader Award created. *Cub Scout Program Helps* included Tiger Cub den meeting plans. Major revision of *Cub Scout Leader Book. Cub Scout Leader How-To Book* rewritten. Cub Scout training award requirements revised, including changes in tenure and adding Youth Protection training. Bob Bedingfield named chairman of national Cub Scout Committee. Bill Steele named associate director of Cub Scout Division.

2002 Age-appropriate guidelines adopted. Leave No Trace Frontcountry Guidelines and Leave No Trace award introduced. All Cub Scouts could now earn the Whittling Chip. Recruiting theme "Fun at Every Turn" featured T.C., Akela, and Baloo. New caps for all ranks. "Power Pack Pals" comics introduced. Alan Westberg named director of Cub Scout Division.

2003 Wolf, Bear, and Webelos handbooks revised. All handbooks had Character Connections activities included as part of advancement requirements. Bobcat requirements changed to include core value of honesty as part of learning Cub Scout Promise. New Fast Start training video created. Don Belcher named chairman of national Cub Scout Committee. Ed Woodlock named associate director of Cub Scout Division.

2004 National "Good Turn for America" launched. Updated Outdoor Skills for Webelos Den Leader training introduced. 75th Anniversary Award and Cub Scout Outdoor Activity Award introduced. Tiger Cub uniform changed to the Cub Scout blue uniform. Hispanic soccer program recruiting emphasis began. Lyle Knight named chairman of the national Cub Scout Committee.

2005 Cub Scouting celebrated 75th Anniversary. Diamond Jubilee theme: "75 Years of Fun, Family, and Friends!"

Appendix 2

CHIEF SCOUT EXECUTIVES AND CUB SCOUT DIVISION DIRECTORS

CHIEF SCOUT EXECUTIVES

Dr. James E. West	1911–43
Dr. Elbert K. Fretwell	1943–48
Dr. Arthur A. Schuck	1948–60
Joseph A. Brunton, Jr.	1960–67
Alden G. Barber	1967–76
Harvey L. Price	1976–79
J. L. Tarr	1979–84
Ben H. Love	1985–93
Jere B. Ratcliffe	1993–2000
Roy L. Williams	2000–

CUB SCOUT DIVISION DIRECTORS

Dr. Huber William Hurt	1930–34
William C. Wessel	1935–49
Gerald A. Speedy	1949–52
O. W. (Bud) Bennett	1952–70
Robert L. Untch	1971–82
Jack Billington	1983–92
Gene Stone	1992–97
G. Richard Williamson	1997–99
Brad Farmer	1999–2002
Alan Westberg	2002–

Appendix 3

THE CHANGING ROLE OF LEADERS

The following shows how the role of leaders in the program has changed over the 75-year history of Cub Scouting.

1930 The first dens were led by Boy Scouts called den chiefs. The dens met in the home of a den member, and the mother was sometimes a helper but not the leader. Pack committee members and Cubmasters were all male.

1932 With the publication of the first *Cubmaster's Packbook* and *Den Chief's Denbook* the den mother was recognized as part of the leadership team, although she was to "share" responsibilities with the den chief, not take charge. On paper, she was merely the liaison between the den and the neighborhood parents' committee.

1936 The National Executive Board approved optional registration of den mothers.

1937 Den mothers were offered a uniform smock.

1938 A badge of office was created for den mothers.

1945 "Cub Scouter" replaced "Cubber" as a term for adult leaders.

1948 All den mothers had to be registered.

1954 The leader of the Webelos den was a man who was registered as an assistant Cubmaster.

1956 The Den Mother's Training Award was introduced to recognize accomplishments of den mothers.

1967 Men as well as women could be registered as Cub Scout den leaders. The title of "den mother" was changed to "den leader" to include both male and female leaders of dens. The den leader coach position was created. Webelos Scouts could go camping accompanied by a male—father, uncle, or family friend.

1969 The first women were named to the national Cub Scout Committee. They were LaVern Parmley and Elizabeth "Betty" Reneker.

1971 The Silver Fawn Award was created for recognizing women at the local council level.

1973 The National Executive Board voted to allow women to serve as institutional representatives, Cub Scout roundtable commissioners, Cub Scout unit commissioners, unit chairmen, and unit committee members, den leaders, assistant den leaders, and den leader coaches. Women also were appointed to area and regional Cub Scouting positions.

1974 The Silver Fawn Award was discontinued as women could now receive the Silver Beaver Award for outstanding service at the council level.

1976 Cub Scout Trainer Wood Badge was introduced for trainers in the Cub Scout program. For the first time, women were allowed to attend the Wood Badge course. Women were now allowed to be Cubmasters and assistant Cubmasters.

1983 Den aides were introduced. This unregistered position was for young people, male and female, who helped with den meetings.

1988 Women were now allowed to be Webelos den leaders and assistant Webelos den leaders.

1992 The Tiger Cub group coach was included in basic training.

1993 The Tiger Cub group coach was included on the pack charter.

2000 The pack trainer position was introduced.

2001 The Tiger Cub den leader position was introduced. The den leader coach position was eliminated.

Index

A

Academics and Sports program, Cub Scout, 77-78, 79, 108, 109
Achievements and electives, 21, 28, 38, 43, 52, 67, 70, 90, 105, 107, 110
Action Book for New Scouts, 70
Action Books, Cub Scout, 70, 107
Activities, inappropriate, 89
Activity badges, Webelos, 43, 68, 70, 106, 108
Adult partner, Tiger Cub, 66, 77, 80, 89, 90, 92
Advancement program, 21, 28, 35, 37, 38, 43, 52, 68, 69, 70, 82, 88, 92
Age- and rank-appropriate guidelines, 91-92
Age-appropriate activities, 80, 88, 91-92
Akela, 6, 10, 11, 88
American Eagles, 8
American Eaglets, 8
American Indian lore, emphasis on, 5, 10, 11
American Tribesmen, 8
Anniversary awards
  50th, 62, 71
  75th, 94, 110
Anniversary, Boy Scouts of America
  50th, 43
  75th, 109
Anniversary, Cub Scouting
  10th, 23
  30th, 105
  50th, 57, 59-62, 107
  55th, 107
  75th, *vii,* 87, 94, 109
Anniversary, World Scouting, 75th, 107
Arrow of Light, chief of the Webelos tribe, 10
Arrow of Light Award, 52, 107
  emblem, 11, 21, 43
  metal badge, 57
  requirements, 68, 82, 88, 92
  square knot, 57, 107
Atkins, Gloria, 108

B

Backyard USA, 105
Baden-Powell, Robert S. S., 5, 6, 55, 61, 103
Badges, activity, 43, 68, 70
Badges of office, 17, 57, 74, 80
Badges of rank, 7, 21, 22, 28, 53, 57, 90
Baloo, 67, 88, 109
BALOO (Basic Adult Leader Outdoor Orientation), 91, 108
Barber, Alden G., 47
Barry, Lyman, 5
Beals, Douglas, 7
Bear Action Book, 70
Bear
  as a rank, 16, 21, 28, 38, 53, 67, 72, 107
  in American Cub Scouting, 10
  in the Cubbing story, 11
Bear Cub Scout Book, 38, 44, 67
Beard, Daniel Carter, 7
Bedingfield, Bob, 108
Behal, Martha Jo, 56
Belcher, Don, 109
Bennett, O. W. "Bud," 35-37, 44, 45, 46, 105, 106
Bicycle Safety program, Cub Scout, 53, 106
Bierer, John M., 27, 104
Big Bear Cub Scout Book, 67, 69, 107
Billington, Jack, 107
Blakey, Tony, 61
Blue and gold banquet, 19, 20, 61, 104
  First national, 107
  Supplies for 75th anniversary, 94
Bobcat, 10, 16, 28, 38, 53, 106
  badge, 57, 90, 106
  pin, 21, 38, 104, 106
  requirements, 21, 79, 88, 92
Bobcat Action Book, 70
Boy Pioneers, 8
Boy Rangers of America, 8, 9, 10
Boys Clubs, 8, 9

Boy's Cubbook, The
Part 1—Wolf Rank, 10, 11, 15, 20, 21
Part 2—Bear Rank, 15-16, 21
Part 3—Lion Rank, 15-16, 21
Boys' Life magazine, 39, 44, 81, 83, 103, 105, 108
Brady, Dr. Rodney H., 51, 107
Braille, books in, 105
British Wolf Cubbing, 5-6, 9, 10, 15
Bronze badges, 22
Brooks, Emerson, 8, 9
Butz, Kenneth, 27

C

Cadet corps, 6
Day camping, 44-45, 79, 80
Day camp
inspection, 55
schools, 55, 69
Camping, 40
day, 44-45, 69
family, 52, 69, 79, 107, 108
overnight, 68, 69, 108
pack, 79, 87, 91, 108
resident, 69, 79
Camporee visits, Webelos, 68
Cannon, Diane, *vii,* 94
Carter, President Jimmy, 61, 62
Catholic Boys Brigade, 9
Character Connections®, 87, 88, 93, 108
"Character Counts—Be Prepared for the 21st Century," 108
Church of Jesus Christ of Latter-Day Saints, 68
Claw, Wolf, 55
"Climb on Safely," 108
Clough, Audrey F., 107
Coffield, H. H., 36, 105
Coleman, Gary, 61
Colors, Webelos, 43, 72, 107
Committee, national Cub Scout, *vii*
first women on, 47
role of, 46-47
Committee, neighborhood, 16
Committee on Cubbing, national, 16
Compass points emblem, 68
Congress of the United States, 104
Core Values, 94
Crime Prevention Award, 79
Crime Prevention, BSA National program, 79
Cub Advancement Record, 104
Cub Leader's Outline, 15, 103
Cub Leaders' Round Table, 18, 19, 27, 29, 30, 31, 103, 104
Cub mother, 6
Cub rings, 6
Cub Scout Academics and Sports Program Guide, 77
Cub Scout and Webelos Scout Program Helps, 82, 83
Cub Scout Ceremonies for Dens and Packs, 83, 108
Cub Scout Family Book, 106
Cub Scout Fun Book, 70, 105
Cub Scout Ideas booklets, 51
Cub Scout Leader Book, 70, 78, 79, 81, 83, 92, 107, 108
Cub Scout Leader How-To Book, 70, 78, 83, 107, 108
Cub Scout Program Helps, 18, 36, 90, 108
Cub Scout Program Quarterly, 36
Cub Scout Roundtable Planning Guide, 90
Cub Scout Songbook, 93
Cub Scout Water Fun Book, 105
Cub Scout/Webelos Scout Award, 62
Cub Scouter Award, 74
Disabilities, Cub Scouts with, 45, 51, 105, 106
Cub units, experimental, 8-11, 15-16, 103
Cubbers, 5
Cubber's Training Award, 19
"Cubbing" becomes "Cub Scouting," 30, 104
Cubbing story, the, 11
Cubmaster Award, 74
Cubmaster's Key, 19
Cubmaster's Packbook, 16, 18, 19, 27, 31, 44, 103
Cubmobile, 18, 21, 104
Cubs of America, 6

D

Davis, Jim, 83
Day Camp School, Cub Scout, 55, 107
Day camp, 44-45, 69, 105, 106, 107
Dehoney, Jerry, 108
Den aides, 117
Den Chief Conference Plan, 105
Den chief conferences, 36
Den Chief Handbook, 107

Den Chief Training, 27, 105
Den chief, 16, 103, 117
Den Chief's Denbook, 16, 103, 105, 117
Den chief's shoulder cord, 104, 107
Den Chief's Training Conference, 105
Den Leader Award, 74
Den leader coach, 44, 106, 109, 117
Den Leader Coach Award, 74
Den leader, 44, 55, 88, 105, 106, 109, 117
Den mother, 16, 31, 44
    badge, 104
    position recognized, 17
    registration, 17, 31
    role of, 17
    uniforms, 17
Den Mother's Denbook, 17, 19, 27, 104, 105
Den Mother's Training Award, 40, 46, 105
Dewey, John, 9
Diamond Jubilee theme, 109
Dievendorf, Laurie O., 56
Dinners, Cub Scout, 18
Disabilities, boys with, 45, 51, 105

E

Elective and achievement changes, 52
Elliott, William, 56
Emergency Preparedness BSA, 87
Ethics in Action, 77, 78, 108
Experimental Cub units, 103

F

Family Action Book, 70
Family Activity Book, 66, 93, 108
Family Activity Packet, Tiger Cubs BSA, 66
Family Award, 62
Family Book, BSA, 79
Family Forum, 61, 107
Family Vacation Training Project, 107
Fang, Wolf, 55
Farmer, Brad, 108
Fast Start training, 67, 73, 80, 81, 90, 108, 109
Finley, Dr. John Huston, 9, 103
Flag emblem, 57
Flanders, Donald H., 51
Florida National High Adventure Sea Base conferences, 82
For God and Country, 105
Fort A. P. Hill, 107
Fretwell, Dr. Elbert Kitlay, 9, 10
Frickel, George C., 105
Fun at Every Turn, 88, 109

G

Garfield, official Cub Scouting "spokescat," 83
Gibson, Robert N., 36, 105
Giles, W. Boyd, 107
Gilwell Park Training Center, 55
God and Family emblem, 106
Golden Anniversary of Cub Scouting, *vii,* 61, 107
Good Turns, 28-29, 30, 35, 40, 62, 74, 87
Good Turns for America, 87, 109
Go-See-Its, 90
Grade and age requirements, 68
Grand howl, 17
Great Depression, 15
Griffin, Mark, 109
Group Meeting Sparklers, 88, 93
Guide to Safe Scouting, 79, 91, 108
Guidebook for Packs, 107
Gustke, Mrs. Charles, 19

H

Harold G. Dye, 7
Hauser, Sue, vii
Hesser, Edmond T., 44, 45, 52, 53, 106
Hispanic outreach, 93
Honor arrow points, 22
Hoover, Dave, 37
Horn, Dr. John C., *vii,* 35, 46-47
Horn, Solveig Wald, 56
How Book of Cubbing, The, 18, 27, 104
How to Protect Your Children from Child Abuse and
    Drug Abuse: A Parent's Guide, 72, 78
Hummel, Peter W., 51, 107
Hurt committee, 103, 104
Hurt, Dr. Huber William, 8-9, 10, 16, 17, 103

I

Immediate recognition emblem, Tiger Cub, 90
Immediate Recognition Kit, 53, 106
Inner-City/Rural program, 51
International Cub Leaders' Conference, 104
"It Happened to Me," 78, 108

J

Jackson, William J., 106
Jamboree, first, 103
Jenks, Dr. Jeremiah W., 103
Jenks, Professor Jeremiah Whipple, 9
Johnson, Glendon E., 51, 107
Joining requirements, 5, 53, 65, 106
Jungle Book, The, 6, 10, 67
Junior Christian Endeavor, 9
Junior Scouts, 5, 6, 8
Junior troops, 5, 6

K

Kennedy, Burts J., *vii,* 70, 107
Kennedy, Frank Brittain, 43, 105
Kipling, Rudyard, 6, 10
KISMIF (Keep It Simple, Make It Fun, 19
Knight, Elizabeth Augustus, 56
Knight, Lyle R., vii, 109
Kuryla, William, vii

L

Law of the Pack, 17, 20, 37
Leader training, 16, 19, 40, 46, 55, 73-74, 81-82, 90, 91
Leaders, role of, 117
Leadership, 16
Leadership Development kit, Cub Scout, 106
Learn-to-Swim program, 54, 106
Leave No Trace, 87, 72, 109
Leave No Trace Awareness Award, 92
Levy, Sol G., 7
Lion rank, 10, 11, 21, 103, 104, 105, 106
Lion–Webelos Book, 37, 105
Literature, Cub Scouting, 7, 10, 11, 18, 20, 27, 35, 45, 62, 70, 82-83, 88, 92, 97, 104, 105, 107
Woodcraft Indians, Little Lodge of, 5
Living Circle, 17, 21, 97
Long Range Planning Committee for Cub Scouting, 107
Luckett, Helen Hart, 56
Lyle Knight, vii, 109

M

Martin, E. S., 9
Membership figures, 6, 16, 22, 27, 31, 40, 43, 47, 57, 67, 83
Membership requirements, 31
Metta emblem, 106
Miller, Kenneth L., 106
Minority youth outreach, 51
Mohawks, 8
Mohegans, 8
Mothers' neighborhood committee, 16
Motto, Cub Scout, 6, 21
"Mr. Cub Scouting," 35
Mugrage, Diane F., 56
Murray, William D., 8, 27, 103, 104

N

Nally, Ann W., *vii,* 56, 57, 62
Nally, James D., vii
National office location, 107
National Den Award, 79, 109
Nelson, C. Joseph, 106
New Leader Essentials, 91

O

One-Star Cub, 6
Onward for God and My Country, 105
Outdoor program, 69, 79, 80, 91-92
Outdoor Program Award, 94
Outdoor Leader Skills for Webelos Den Leaders, 91
Outreach to the poor, minority youth, and boys with disabilities, 51

P

Pack Award, 62
Pack Committee pamphlet, 105
Pack Financial Record Book, 18, 104
Pack meetings, 17

Pack Thrift Plan, 18, 104
Pack trainer, 90, 117
Parent meetings, 17
Parent Review Party Kit, 106
Parents' Cub Book, 15, 103
Parmley, LaVern W., 46, 47, 56, 57, 117
Parry, Donald J., 51, 106
Pauline Chaulker, 7
Phillips, Waite, 104
Philmont conferences for Cub Scout leaders, first, 40
Philmont Scout Ranch, 11, 40, 104, 105, 106
Physical Fitness pin, 71
Physical Fitness, Cub Scout, 45, 53, 106
Physical Fitness, National Cub Scout Championship, 53
Pinewood derby, 35, 38, 39, 45, 105
Poor youth, outreach to, 51
Post, Marjorie Meriweather, 56
Pow Wow Guide, 46
Pow wows, first, 19
Power Pack Pals, 93, 109
Prepared for Today, 70
President's Energy Award, 62
Program expansion, 65, 68-69
Program year change, 106
Progress Toward Rank emblem, 53
Project SOAR, 54, 106
Promise, Cub Scout, 20, 37, 52
Public Relations Plan, 107
Publications, electronic, 83
Purpose of Cub Scouting, 44
Purposes of Cub Scouting, 89

Q

Quality Unit Award, 74, 78
Quarterly Leadership Updates, 81, 108

R

Raingutter regattas, 39
Ranks in Cub Scouting, 6, 107
Reaves, Sam, 15
Regattas for model boats, 35
Reneker, Elizabeth "Betty" C., 46, 47, 117
Requirement changes, 92
Requirements for Bear, first, 21
Requirements for Bobcat, first, 21
Requirements for Lion, first, 21
Requirements for Wolf, first, 21
Robinson, E. O. "Robbie," 74, 107
Rocket Derby, 54
Rogers, Jack, 62
Round Table, Cub Leaders, 18
Rounds, Mary Anne, *vii,* 56
Roundtables, monthly, 31

S

Salute, Cub, 20
Sanford, Augusta L., 56
Save Our American Resources, 54, 106
Schiff Scout Reservation, 19, 22, 103, 106
Schmidt, Ernie, 45
Schneider, Richard, 61
School Night for Scouting Plan, 83
Scott, Jack, 107
Scouter's Key, 46
Scouter's Training Award, 46
Scouting for Boys, 6
Scouting magazine, 104
Scouting, differences from Cubbing, 22
Scouting—A Bridge to the Future, 108
Seamans, C. Walter, 9, 10, 22, 104
Seig, Marlin S., 106
September 11, 2001, 87
Seton library and museum, 11
Seton, Ernest Thompson, 5, 6, 9, 10, 11, 16,
Sherman, Jason Roger, 61
Shumway, Naomi, 56
Sieg, Marlin, 36, 39, 40, 105
Sign, Cub Scout, 20
Silver Antelope Award, 56, 57
Silver Beaver Award, 56, 57, 103, 107, 117
Silver Buffalo Award, 11, 57, 103
Silver Fawn Award, 56, 57, 106, 117
Sixer, 6
Sixes, 6, 9
Skinner, Sam, 108
Soccer and Scouting, 93
"So You're a New Cubmaster," 73

"So You're a New Den Leader," 73
"So You're a New Pack Committee Member," 73
"So You're a New Webelos Den Leader," 73
Space Derby, 45
Spanish-language literature, 93
Speedy, Gerald A., 27, 104
Sports and Physical Fitness Program, Cub Scout, 70-71
Sports electives, 105
Sports letter, 71
Sports pin, 71, 77
Spotlight on New and Updated Cub Scout Program Elements, 82
Spotlight on Pow Wow, 93
Steele, William, 108
Stewart, William, vii
Storefront Scout centers, 51
Strang, Edmund D., 15
Strong Values—Strong Leaders, 77
Summer Program pamphlet, 27
Symbolism in Cub Scouting, 20

T

T.C., 81, 88, 109
Tenderpad, 6
10 Steps to Pack Organization, 105
Terms, Cub Scouting, 10
Boys Cubbook, The 11
Themes, BSA national, 77, 105
Themes, monthly, 17, 18, 27
Thomas, Ernest R. "Tommy" Jr., *vii,* 68, 78, 107
Tiger Cub belt totem, 80, 90
Tiger Cub coach, 80, 108, 109
Tiger Cub Den Leader Award, 108
Tiger Cub den leader, 90, 108, 117
Tiger Cub emblem, 67, 109
Tiger Cub group coach, 80, 108, 117
Tiger Cub Group Coach Award, 108
Tiger Cub Guidebook, 67, 80
Tiger Cub Handbook, 89-90
Tiger Cub program changes, 89-90
Tiger Cub rank, 87
Tiger Cub Resource Book, 81
Tiger Cub uniform, 90, 109
Tiger Cubs BSA, 51, 80-81
Tiger Cubs, BSA, 65, 107
Tiger Mania, 81, 108
Tiger Tracks, 67, 107
Trained Leader emblem, 73
Trainer Development Conference, 91
Training 2000 Award, 82, 108
Training, leader, 16, 19, 39-40, 46, 55, 73, 81-82, 90-91, 104
Turner, Russ, 45
Two-deep leadership, 72
Two-Star Cub, 6

U

Uniform, 20, 28, 31, 43, 57, 61, 65, 72
Unit Leadership Enhancements, 81, 108
University of Scouting, 91
Untch, Robert L., 36, 51, 106, 107

Values, positive, 88

W

War effort, Cub Scouts helping with, 28-29, 30
Weaver, Ray L., 22
Webelos
    den concept, 37
    meaning of, 21
Webelos Award, 43, 52
Webelos Den Activities, 70, 82
Webelos Den Book, 38, 105
Webelos Den Leader Award, 74
Webelos Leader Guide, 82
Webelos Scout Book, 68, 107
Webelos Scout
    program, 43
    rank, 28
Webelos Woods, 69, 107
Weierman, Sue, 88
Wells, Kenneth A., 44, 105
Wendelin, Rudy, 61
Wessel, William C., 22, 104, 105
West, James E., 5, 7, 9, 11, 22, 27, 103
Westberg, Alan, *vii,* 109
Whittling Chip, 67, 108, 109

Williams, Roy L., *vi*
Williams, Russell A. Jr., 107
Wills, J. Bowling, 106
Wolf Action Book, 70
Wolf Cubbing, 6, 7
Wolf Cubbook, 21
Wolf Cub packs, first, 6
Wolf Cub Scout Book, 68
Wolf Cub's Handbook (British), 6, 7, 103
Wolf in the Cubbing story, 11
Wolf requirements, 21
Women, role of in Cub Scouting, 31, 40, 44, 46, 47, 56, 57, 69, 104, 105, 106, 177
Wood Badge for the 21st Century, 91, 108
Wood Badge, 55, 56, 90, 109, 117
Woodcraft Indians, 5, 8, 9, 10, 11
Woodlock, Ed, 107, 109
Woodman, 6
World Crest emblem, 107
World War II, 27, 28-29, 30, 35, 40, 47

Y

YMCA, 9
"Younger boy problem," 5, 8
Youth Protection training, 71, 72, 74, 77, 78-79, 108